Historic Supreme Court Decisions

McDougal Littell
A HOUGHTON MIFFLIN COMPANY

Evanston, Illinois • Boston • Dallas

Contents

Supreme Court Decision 1

Marbury v. Madison (1803)
Teacher Lesson Plan

Rationale

This lesson is designed to explore with students the growing role of the federal judiciary in the early 1800s. Under the leadership of Chief Justice John Marshall, the Supreme Court made several decisions that strengthened the new national government and established its role in interpreting national law. This landmark case was the first in which the Court assumed the right to declare an act of Congress unconstitutional, providing the basis for the concept of judicial review.

General Goals

This case study will provide students with opportunities to:

1. explore the challenges of American constitutional law
2. understand the processes and procedures of the judicial system
3. examine the role of the Supreme Court in the formation of public policy
4. explore the conflict between judicial activism and judicial restraint
5. examine the opinions of Supreme Court justices
6. demonstrate critical thinking skills

Directions

Student material is provided in four blackline masters on the following pages. These should be copied and distributed to students. They include a brief description of *Marbury v. Madison* as well as questions for students to answer.

Elements of the Case presents questions to check student comprehension, providing an opportunity to review with students the central issues, the Court's decision and rationale, and the effects of the case.

Evaluation of the Case provides one or more critical thinking activities for students. In this section, students are asked to evaluate the case and express their own positions on its issues.

Answer Key and Extending the Lesson

An answer key for the questions is provided on the next page, along with suggested activities for extending the lesson.

Marbury v. Madison (1803)

Answer Key

Elements of the Case

1. *Issue:* Should the Court issue a writ of mandamus ordering the Secretary of State to deliver the commission to Marbury and the others?
2. Marbury contended he was entitled to his commission because (1) the Senate had approved the commission, (2) President Adams had signed it, and (3) the Secretary of State had placed the seal of the United States on it. Madison, the new Secretary of State, contended that he was entitled to withhold the commission because it had not been delivered.
3. By unanimous vote the Court rejected Marbury's petition. They agreed that he was entitled to his commission and that a court could order it but argued that the Supreme Court did not have the right to issue such an order. Their power to do so came from an act of Congress that was unconstitutional.
4. The Supreme Court, for the first time, declared an act of Congress void on the grounds that it violated the Constitution. The decision established the U.S. Supreme Court as the final authority on the meaning and interpretation of the Constitution.

Evaluation of the Case

1. Answers will vary, as historians disagree about the framers' intent or whether Marshall simply assumed this power by this decision.
2. Answers will vary, because judicial review of acts of Congress is seen as an important power of the Court. However, some experts point out that few other governments give their courts such power and that the Court has in fact overturned relatively few acts of Congress. It has ruled more often on the unconstitutionality of state statutes, which was not an issue here.
3. The legal requirements had been met by Senate approval, the President's signature, and the sealing of the document. Delivery was of no consequence at all.

Extending the Lesson

1. Several strong and interesting historical personalities played a role in this case, including John Marshall, Thomas Jefferson, and James Madison. Have students research biographical information on these men and trace their political and personal relationships.
2. President Thomas Jefferson, a political and personal enemy of John Marshall, harshly criticized the Marbury decision. It was his view that each department (legislative, executive, judicial) was responsible for determining the constitutionality of its own actions. Given this view, ask students to discuss the consequences for the country if this were true. In practical terms, how much do the departments interfere with one another? How does this relate to the checks and balances system described in the U.S. Constitution?
3. A good video reenactment of the *Marbury* case is included in the series "Equal Justice Under Law," funded by the Commission on the Bicentennial of the U.S. Constitution, chaired by Warren G. Burger. The video, *Marbury v. Madison,* is distributed by National Audio Visual Center, 8700 Edgeworth Drive, Capital Heights, Maryland, 20743-3701.

Marbury v. Madison (1803)

Vocabulary

lame duck Referring to officeholders who have not been re-elected and so serve the remainder of their term in office with little backing or authority.

commission Official document authorizing certain duties and powers.

petition In law, a formal, written request to a court asking for a specific action.

writ of mandamus A court order requiring a government official to carry out his or her official duty.

dilemma Difficult choice between two relatively equal options.

original jurisdiction The authority of a court to be the first to hear and decide a case.

appellate jurisdiction The right of a court to hear a case "on appeal" after the original court has acted.

Reviewing the Case

With the election of 1800, for the first time political parties played an active role in American government. The Federalists supported President John Adams while the Republicans supported Vice President Thomas Jefferson. Each party had its own agenda, based on different governing philosophies and different viewpoints about the Constitution.

In the election, the Federalists lost the presidency and control of both houses of Congress. The only branch of government in which they could exercise any power was the judiciary. Understanding this, the Federalists worked out a strategy to strengthen their hold on the federal courts.

Presidential inaugurations were then in March, giving the **"lame duck"** Federalists several months. Before the inauguration and the start of the new Republican-dominated Congress, the Federalist Congress passed the Judiciary Act of 1801, which created 62 new judgeships. John Adams, the outgoing President, quickly filled the new jobs with avid Federalists, and the Senate approved his ap-pointments. Late into the night of March 3, 1801, Adams was still signing the **commissions** of these last-minute nominations. They were sealed with the Seal of the United States by the outgoing Secretary of State and were then to be delivered to the new officials by a State Department clerk. Because of the last-minute rush, not all the commissions could be delivered before Jefferson took office as President on March 4, 1801.

When he learned about the commissions of the "midnight judges," as they were called, Jefferson angrily ordered the commissions withheld. One of the late commissions was for William Marbury, who had been named as a justice of the peace in the District of Columbia. Marbury refused to be denied his job. He convinced three others to accompany him to the State Department, but he was still refused his commission. Marbury then turned to the United States Supreme Court and **petitioned** it for a **writ of mandamus**, which would order the new Secretary of State, James Madison, to deliver the commission or show just cause for not doing so.

Marbury's petition resulted in one of the most significant decisions in the history of the Supreme Court. The issue before the Court: Should the Court issue a writ of mandamus ordering the Secretary of State to deliver commissions to Marbury and the others who had been denied?

The Supreme Court, by unanimous vote, turned down Marbury's request for the court order. Although the justices agreed that Marbury was legally entitled to the commission, the Court would not order the Secretary of State to give it to him. Why not?

Writing for the Court, Chief Justice John Marshall explained the position:

> Mr. Marbury, then, since his commission was signed by the President, and sealed by the Secretary of State, was appointed. . . . To withhold his commission, therefore, is an act deemed by the court not warranted by law, but violative of a vested legal right.

The question was not Marbury's right to have the job, but the Court's own constitutional authority. The case had created a **dilemma** for the Court.

On the one hand, if the Court ruled in favor of Marbury and issued the writ, the new administration under Jefferson most likely would ignore it. That would make the Supreme Court look weak, emphasizing the fact that the Court had no way to enforce its decisions. For that, it had to rely on the executive branch—the people to whom the order applied.

On the other hand, deciding *not* to issue the writ also would make the Court look weak. It would appear as if the Court were avoiding its duty by giving in to the executive branch.

How could the Court disentangle itself from such a treacherous decision? Marshall turned to the Constitution itself to point out that it did not give the Court **original jurisdiction** in a case like this:

The Constitution vests the whole judicial power of the United States in one Supreme Court, and such inferior courts as Congress shall from time to time, ordain and establish. . . . In the distribution of this power it is declared that "the Supreme Court shall have original jurisdiction in all cases affecting ambassadors, other public ministers and consuls, and those in which a state shall be a party. In all other cases, the Supreme Court shall have **appellate jurisdiction**." . . . To enable the Court, then, to issue a mandamus, it must be shown to be an exercise of appellate jurisdiction.

Since Marbury's case had not come from a lower court, the Supreme Court could not act, Marshall said. In addition, its power to issue such writs to public officers came from an Act of Congress, not the Constitution. In structuring the federal courts, Congress had passed the Judiciary Act of 1789, which gave the Supreme Court expanded original powers beyond the Constitution. In following this line of reasoning, Marshall then was faced with the question of what to do about an act of Congress that violated the Constitution.

His explanation established an important principle:

. . . there is no middle ground. The Constitution is either a superior paramount law, unchangeable by ordinary means, or it is on a level with ordinary legislative acts, and, like other acts, is alterable when the legislature shall please to alter it. If the former part . . . be true, then a legislative act contrary to the Constitution is not law: if the latter part be true, then written constitutions are absurd attempts, on the part of people, to limit a power in its nature illimitable. . . .

It is emphatically the province and duty of the judicial department to say what the law is. . . . So if a law be in opposition to the Constitution; if both the law and the Constitution apply to a particular case . . . the court must determine which of these conflicting rules governs the case. This is the very essence of judicial duty. . . .

Thus the particular phraseology [wording] of the Constitution of the United States confirms and strengthens the principle, supposed to be essential to all written constitutions, that a law repugnant to the Constitution is void. . . .

The long-term significance of this case was Marshall's use of the Constitution to give the Supreme Court the power of judicial review, even though that was not the original issue. While the justices agreed that Marbury was entitled to his court order, the act of Congress that would allow them to issue it went beyond the Constitution. It was the first time the Court openly declared an act of Congress unconstitutional and claimed the right to be the final authority on the meaning of the U.S. Constitution. Judicial review was not used again by the Court in regard to Congress for another 54 years, but in the twentieth century it became a powerful tool for influencing public policy.

Name _____ Date _____

Marbury v. Madison (1803)

Elements of the Case

Directions: Fill in the appropriate information for each of the following elements of this case.

1. State the issue before the Supreme Court in this case.

_____

_____

_____

_____

2. What facts of the case were presented to the Court?

_____

_____

_____

_____

3. What was the decision of the Court? What was the rationale behind it?

_____

_____

_____

_____

4. What was the effect of the decision?

_____

_____

_____

_____

Evaluation of the Case

Directions: Use your own judgment to evaluate the justices' decision and state your opinion of that decision.

1. Do you think the framers of the Constitution intended the Supreme Court to have the power of judicial review as part of the system of "checks and balances"? Explain.

_____

_____

_____

_____

_____

_____

2. What would be the effect on the United States if this decision had not validated the idea that the Supreme Court has the power to judge whether acts of Congress are unconstitutional?

_____

_____

_____

_____

_____

3. According to Justice Marshall, what actions were necessary to make the commissions legal? Was it the delivery of the commissions or was it the process of Senate approval, the President's signature, and the official seal by the Secretary of State? Why was this an important point?

_____

_____

_____

_____

_____

Supreme Court Decision 2

United States v. Judge Peters (1809)
Teacher Lesson Plan

Rationale

This lesson is designed to explore with students the growing role of the federal judiciary in the early 1800s. Under the leadership of Chief Justice John Marshall, the Supreme Court made a number of decisions that strengthened the new national government and established its role in interpreting national law. This Supreme Court case established the constitutional right of federal courts to enforce their decisions over the will of state legislatures.

General Goals

This case study will provide students with opportunities to:

1. explore the challenges of American constitutional law
2. understand the processes and procedures of the judicial system
3. examine the role of the Supreme Court in the formation of public policy
4. explore the conflict between judicial activism and judicial restraint
5. examine the opinions of Supreme Court justices
6. demonstrate critical thinking skills

Directions

Student material is provided in four blackline masters on the following pages. These should be copied and distributed to students. They include a brief description of the *Judge Peters* case as well as questions for students to answer.

Elements of the Case presents questions to check student comprehension, providing an opportunity to review with students the central issues, the Court's decision and rationale, and the effects of the case.

Evaluation of the Case provides one or more critical thinking activities for students. In this section, students are asked to evaluate the case and express their own positions on its issues.

Answer Key and Extending the Lesson

An answer key for the questions is provided on the next page, along with suggested activities for extending the lesson.

United States v. Judge Peters (1809)

Answer Key

Elements of the Case

1. *Issue:* Can a state legislature legally pass a law that overrules a decision of the courts of the United States?

2. In a dispute over proceeds from a captured ship, a national appeals committee (named by Congress) and a Pennsylvania state court disagreed. A federal district court, under Judge Richard Peters, ordered the money to be paid to one claimant; but the state legislature passed an act claiming the money for the state and authorizing the governor to use force to resist. The U.S. Supreme Court ordered payment, but Judge Peters delayed, hoping the state legislature would cancel the law and thereby avoid a confrontation between the state of Pennsylvania and the United States.

3. The Court ordered Judge Peters to turn over the proceeds to Olmstead, thus upholding the ruling of the Committee (named by Congress). The ruling enforced the decisions of a national government agency and the federal courts over an act passed by a state legislature.

4. The long-term effects of the decision meant that a state legislature does not have the right to pass laws that overrule the decisions of federal courts. This decision helped establish the supremacy of national laws.

Evaluation of the Case

1. Answers will vary, but most students are likely to sympathize with the sailors who actually brought the ship in—both Olmstead's group and the crews of the two American ships.

2. Answers should show that students grasp the distinction that two different levels of government and court systems are involved here. If federal courts did not have this power, they could not maintain the supremacy of national law.

3. Answers should reflect students' understanding that this period of lawmaking had a permanent effect in establishing the role of the Supreme Court. Other decisions that contributed include *Marbury*, *McCulloch*, and *Gibbons v. Ogden*.

Extending the Lesson

1. Richard Peters was a prominent and influential jurist and public official, who was active in many areas in this period of history. Another person who figured in this case was David Rittenhouse, who was a well-known scientist as well as a public official. Have some students research the life of these two interesting people.

2. There have been a number of contemporary situations in which states have resisted or defied federal court orders or other federal rulings. Discuss with students hypothetical and actual situations; e.g.,(1) court-ordered public school integration; (2) state refusal to allow the national guard to be called to duty; (3) prayer in schools; (4) refusal to pay taxes; (5) federal bans against discrimination in employment or housing.

United States v. Judge Peters (1809)

Vocabulary

admiralty Branch of law dealing with naval matters and the law of the sea.

executor Person appointed to carry out the provisions of another's will and manage his or her estate.

Reviewing the Case

Knowing that the American Revolution would cause conflicts concerning the rightful ownership of captured prizes of war, the Continental Congress in 1777 named a Committee of Appeals to review any such conflicts. The right of this national authority to decide cases was challenged, however, in the case that was eventually decided in *United States v. Judge Peters* (1809).

In 1778, a British sloop, the *Active,* was on its way from Jamaica to New York, carrying supplies for British soldiers in New York. On board were Gideon Olmstead and other men from Connecticut, who had been imprisoned by the British and forced to work as seamen on the vessel. During the voyage, Olmstead and the other American prisoners managed to seize control of the ship. Hoping to reach a safe port, they headed for Egg Harbor, in the colony of New Jersey. But as they neared port, the *Active* was captured by the American ship *Convention,* registered in Pennsylvania. The *Active* was taken to Philadelphia, where the captain of the *Convention* claimed it as a prize of war. Olmstead and the others also claimed the *Active* and its cargo.

The Pennsylvania Court of **Admiralty** ordered the ship and cargo sold. Three fourths of the proceeds were to be divided among the crews of the *Convention* and the *Le Gerald,* an American privateer. The crew of the *Le Gerald* claimed a share on the grounds that their ship, too, was in sight of the *Active* at the time of its capture and was in pursuit.

Gideon Olmstead and the others who had first taken possession of the *Active* were given only a one-fourth share. Believing this was unfair, they petitioned Congress, which sent the case to the Committee of Appeals. The Committee represented the national government. After a hearing, the Committee reversed the decision of the state admiralty court and ruled that Olmstead and his group were entitled to all the proceeds from the *Active.* The case went back to the state court, but the Pennsylvania judge refused to pay the proceeds to either party. Instead, he placed the money in the hands of David Rittenhouse, the state treasurer of Pennsylvania, who kept the funds and the interest growing from then until his death in 1796. In his own handwriting, Rittenhouse had left instructions that upon his death, his **executors** were to turn over the money to the state of Pennsylvania as soon as the state took legal responsibility for the money.

In 1803, after years of legal proceedings, Judge Richard Peters of the district court ruled that the Rittenhouse estate should turn over the money to Olmstead. The Pennsylvania legislature, however, passed an act claiming the money for the state and authorizing the governor to resist—by force if necessary—any attempt by the courts of the United States to take possession of the money.

Tensions over the case continued. In 1808, Olmstead (by then in his 80s) petitioned the Supreme Court of the United States. He obtained a court order instructing Judge Peters to tell the Rittenhouse estate to release the money. To avoid a showdown between state and federal forces, however, Judge Peters did not follow these instructions. He hoped, instead, that the Pennsylvania legislature would cancel the act, avoiding the confrontation that seemed likely. The governor of Pennsylvania was ready to call out some 1,400 armed men of the state militia. Federal marshals were arming a posse of about 2,000.

Peters agreed to issue that order if the Supreme Court so ruled. The issue before the court: Can a state legislature legally pass a law that overrules a decision of the courts of the United States?

The Supreme Court ruled against the state of Pennsylvania, ordering that the money be paid to Olmstead. This upheld the original rulings of both the Committee of Appeals (named by Congress) and the federal district court. It established the principle that a state legislature does not have the right to overrule the federal courts. In the opinion, Chief Justice John Marshall stated:

If the legislatures of the several states may, at will, annul the judgments of the courts of the United States, and destroy the rights acquired under those judgments, the constitution itself becomes a solemn mockery, and the nation is deprived of the means of enforcing its own tribunals.

The significance of the decision was Marshall's assertion that the federal courts must be superior to the state legislatures in order to preserve the new nation and the supremacy of national law. Without this authority, the states would not have to follow rulings made by the national courts.

Supreme Court Decision 2

Name _____ Date _____

United States v. Judge Peters (1809)

Elements of the Case

Directions: Fill in the appropriate information for each of the following elements of this case.

1. State the issue before the Supreme Court in this case.

_____

_____

_____

_____

_____

2. What facts of the case were presented to the Court?

_____

_____

_____

_____

_____

3. What was the decision of the Court? What was the rationale behind it?

_____

_____

_____

_____

4. What was the effect of the decision?

_____

_____

_____

_____

Evaluation of the Case

Directions: Use your own judgment to evaluate the justices' decision and state your opinion of that decision.

1. In your opinion, should the state have received the money or should Gideon Olmstead and the others have received it? Explain.

_____

_____

_____

_____

_____

2. What do you think would be the consequences if a state legislature could overrule decisions made by federal courts? Explain.

_____

_____

_____

_____

_____

3. Do you think an issue such as this would arise today? What Supreme Court decisions enforced the idea of the supremacy of the Constitution and national law? Explain.

_____

_____

_____

_____

_____

Supreme Court Decision 3

McCulloch v. Maryland (1819)
Teacher Lesson Plan

Rationale

This lesson is designed to explore with students the growing role of the federal judiciary in the early 1800s. Under the leadership of Chief Justice John Marshall, the Supreme Court made a number of decisions that strengthened the new national government and established its role in interpreting national law. This landmark case also confirmed congressional use of the implied powers clause ("elastic clause") in the Constitution.

General Goals

This case study will provide students with opportunities to:

1. explore the challenges of American constitutional law
2. understand the processes and procedures of the judicial system
3. examine the role of the Supreme Court in the formation of public policy
4. explore the conflict between judicial activism and judicial restraint
5. examine the opinions of Supreme Court justices
6. demonstrate critical thinking skills

Directions

Student material is provided in four blackline masters on the following pages. These should be copied and distributed to students. They include a brief description of *McCulloch v. Maryland* as well as questions for students to answer.

Elements of the Case presents questions to check student comprehension, providing an opportunity to review with students the central issues, the Court's decision and rationale, and the effects of the case.

Evaluation of the Case provides one or more critical thinking activities for students. In this section, students are asked to evaluate the case and express their own positions on its issues.

Answer Key and Extending the Lesson

An answer key for the questions is provided on the next page, along with suggested activities for extending the lesson.

McCulloch v. Maryland (1819)

Answer Key

Elements of the Case

1. *Issue:* Does any state possess the constitutional right to tax an agency of the United States government? Another issue in this case was whether Congress could constitutionally establish a national bank.

2. The state of Maryland felt that the Constitution allowed states to tax agencies of the federal government because the only specific restriction (Article I, Section 10) on the states' power to tax was related to imports and exports. The state also questioned the right of the Congress to create the Bank of United States and to place branches in the various states without legislative approval. McCulloch and the United States attorney felt no state could tax the United States or any agency of it. To do so would allow the state legislatures to become sovereign over the national government, which represented the people as a whole. They contended that Congress had the right to create the bank under the "implied powers" clause of the Constitution (Article I, Section 8, Clause 18).

3. The Court ruled unanimously in favor of McCulloch, saying the state legislatures had no right to tax the national government, that the national laws passed by Congress are superior when in conflict with state statutes (Article VI). The Court also found that Congress had the constitutional right to create a national bank as part of its "implied powers."

4. The long-term effect of the case established the principle that national law would be superior to state law whenever the two come into conflict. Equally important, it recognized a broad definition of the "implied powers," strengthening the powers of Congress and the national government.

Evaluation of the Case

1. Answers will vary but should show that students understand the implications of having the power or authority to impose a tax.

2. Answers should point out that Congress includes representatives from all states, who are elected to represent the country as a whole; state legislators represent the people of a single state. Students may agree or disagree, pointing out that members of Congress also are elected from the states.

3. Students should understand that this case was an important step in establishing a "loose interpretation" of the elastic clause.

Extending the Lesson

1. Have students discuss some applications of this decision. For instance, can a state impose income taxes on interest from U.S. Treasury bills or U.S. savings bonds? Why not? On the other hand, could the Montana legislature make it legal to kill a bald eagle in the state of Montana after the federal Bureau of Fish and Wildlife had banned such action by placing the bird on the endangered species list?

2. A good video reenactment of the *McCulloch* case is included in the series "Equal Justice Under Law," funded by the Commission on the Bicentennial of the U.S. Constitution, chaired by Warren G. Burger. The video, *McCulloch v. Maryland*, is distributed by National Audio Visual Center, 8700 Edgeworth Drive, Capital Heights, Maryland, 20743-3701.

McCulloch v. Maryland (1819)

Vocabulary

real property Land or buildings, real estate.

implied powers Powers of the national government that are not specified in the Constitution but are based on the "necessary and proper" clause (elastic clause), which gives Congress authority to carry out its specified functions.

delegated powers Powers specifically granted to the national government in the Constitution.

sovereignty A state or nation's authority to govern itself.

Reviewing the Case

The early 1800s were years in which the United States faced unfamiliar situations concerning federalism and the division of authority between the national government and the various state governments. Such questions were often taken to court for definition and interpretation. Some of the decisions made then have had a lasting impact on how the country is governed. One of these early landmark cases is *McCulloch v. Maryland*, which arose in 1819.

In April 1816, Congress chartered the Second National Bank of the United States. This bank was the successor to the first Bank of the United States, started through the efforts of Alexander Hamilton. The original charter had expired in 1811 and was not immediately renewed because of questions about the constitutionality of a national bank. Many people objected to both the idea and the existence of a national bank. They thought it harmed state economies and local businesses and gave the national government too much power. The Second National Bank was in Philadelphia, with branch offices in other states. One branch was in Baltimore, Maryland.

On February 11, 1818, the Maryland state assembly passed an act aimed specifically at the Second National Bank. It imposed a "stamp tax" on the paper that banks used in printing bank notes. All banks not chartered by the state had to pay either a tax to obtain the special stamped paper or an annual state tax of $15,000. Each violation would result in a fine of $500 for the bank and a $100 fine for each individual responsible.

James McCulloch, cashier of the Baltimore branch, refused to pay the tax, despite repeated notices from the state. The state of Maryland brought suit against him in the County Court of Baltimore and later appealed to the State Court of Appeals, where McCulloch lost.

On behalf of himself and the U.S. government, McCulloch then brought the case to the Supreme Court in an attempt to reverse the decision. As it came to the Supreme Court, the issue became: Does any state have the constitutional right to tax an agency of the United States government?

Some of the most famous lawyers of the time argued the case. The attorneys for the state of Maryland argued that a state did have the right to tax because it was not forbidden by Article I, Section 10, of the Constitution, which lists the powers denied to the states. The only restrictions on the state's power to tax, they said, were those specifically mentioned. Those limits concern mainly imports and exports. The state also questioned the right of the Congress to create a national bank and to place branches in the various states without legislative approval.

The lawyers for the United States government argued that the states were forbidden to tax anything of the national government beyond **real property** that the national government owned in the states. They stated that the power of the state to tax the Second National Bank or any other agency of the national government would create the power to destroy the national government.

The Supreme Court decided on behalf of McCulloch, defining two issues of constitutional law:

First, the Court found that creating a national bank was within the **implied powers** of Congress, based on Article I, Section 8, of the Constitution. The final clause of Article I gives Congress the power to pass the legislation needed, or "necessary and proper," to carry out the other functions for which it is responsible. These are its **delegated powers**. In this instance, the creation of a national bank was necessary in order for Congress to create and coin a national currency, collect taxes, and borrow money in an emergency, among other things. These are delegated powers, specifically granted to Congress alone.

If, however, the act establishing a national bank was constitutional, did the state legislature of Maryland have the right to tax the bank? Citing Article VI of the Constitution, the Court declared that this action violated the principle of the supremacy of the national government over the states. The Court believed that granting individual states the right to tax the national government would in effect place the states in a position of **sovereignty** over the national government.

It would also place the individual states in a position superior to people of the Union collectively. This interpretation would return the country to the turmoil suffered under the Articles of Confederation.

Writing for the Court, Chief Justice John Marshall stated:

It being the opinion of the court that the act incorporating the bank is constitutional, and that the power of establishing a branch in the state of Maryland might be properly exercised by the bank itself, we proceed to inquire: Whether the state of Maryland may, without violation of the Constitution, tax that branch? . . . That the power of taxing it by the states may be exercised so as to destroy it, is too obvious to be denied. . . . We are unanimously of the opinion that the law passed by the legislature of Maryland, imposing a tax on the Bank of the United States, is unconstitutional and void.

The significance of *McCulloch v. Maryland* goes to the very root of the purpose of a federal government, one divided by the Constitution between a central government and state governments. The purpose of such government was "to provide a more perfect union." Limits of power were imposed at both national and state levels, but enough power remained at the national level to carry out what Congress found "necessary and proper" to provide good government for the people of the country as a whole. This decision confirmed the legitimate right of Congress to utilize the implied powers clause in passing laws to carry out its delegated powers. It further declared and validated the supremacy of the people collectively represented by Congress over the powers of individual states.

Name _____   Date _____

McCulloch v. Maryland (1819)

Elements of the Case

Directions: Fill in the appropriate information for each of the following elements of this case.

1. State the issue before the Supreme Court in this case.

_____

_____

_____

_____

2. What facts of the case were presented to the Court?

_____

_____

_____

_____

3. What was the decision of the Court? What was the rationale behind it?

_____

_____

_____

4. What was the effect of the decision?

_____

_____

_____

_____

Supreme Court Decision 3

Evaluation of the Case

Directions: Use your own judgment to evaluate the justices' decision
and state your opinion of that decision.

1. Explain in your own words the meaning of Justice Marshall's statement, "The power to tax is the power to destroy."

   _____

   _____

   _____

   _____

2. Think about the following statement and respond with your opinion.
   To paraphrase Justice Marshall: A tax on the states by the United
   States government is a tax levied on its constituency by their elected
   officials in the Congress, whereas a tax on the United States by a
   state legislature is a tax levied on people who are not all the constitu-
   ents of the legislators of that state. (Keep in mind that a *constituent*
   is a person for whom a government may make laws and to whom
   elected officials are accountable.)

   _____

   _____

   _____

   _____

3. Was the decision in this case an example of the Court's use of "loose
   interpretation" of the Constitution or an example of "strict interpretation"? Explain.

   _____

   _____

   _____

   _____

Supreme Court Decision 4

Gibbons v. Ogden (1824)
Teacher Lesson Plan

Rationale

This lesson is designed to explore with students the growing role of the federal judiciary in the early 1800s. Under the leadership of Chief Justice John Marshall, the Supreme Court made a number of decisions that strengthened the new national government. This landmark Supreme Court case established the national government's control over interstate commerce.

General Goals

This case study will provide students with opportunities to:

1. explore the challenges of American constitutional law
2. understand the processes and procedures of the judicial system
3. examine the role of the Supreme Court in the formation of public policy
4. explore the conflict between judicial activism and judicial restraint
5. examine the opinions of Supreme Court Justices
6. demonstrate critical thinking skills

Directions

Student material is provided in four blackline masters on the following pages. These should be copied and distributed to students. The material includes a brief description of the background and issues in the case of *Gibbons v. Ogden*, as well as questions for students to answer.

Elements of the Case presents questions to check student comprehension, providing an opportunity to review with students the central issues, the Court's decision and rationale, and the effects of the case.

Evaluation of the Case provides one or more critical thinking activities for students. In this section, students are asked to evaluate the case and express their own positions on its issues.

Answer Key and Extending the Lesson

An answer key for the questions is provided on the next page, along with suggested activities for extending the lesson.

Gibbons v. Ogden (1824)

Answer Key

Elements of the Case

1. *Issue:* Do the laws passed by the New York legislature violate the Constitution of the United States by their attempt to regulate interstate commerce or is this a permissible interpretation of the "commerce clause"?

2. Ogden argued that he had an exclusive right to navigate the waters in question because they were in the territory of the state of New York, which had the right to regulate trade within its boundaries.

   Gibbons argued that the state of New York could not interfere because he had been properly licensed by the national government through an act of Congress to operate his steamboats in any waters of the coastal United States.

3. The Court ruled unanimously in favor of Gibbons. The justices based their decision on the argument that commerce included transportation of goods and services as well as the sale or exchange of goods and services. Therefore, Congress had the power to regulate transportation across state lines for purposes of commerce. The Court ruled that the New York law was in conflict with a constitutional act of Congress and was for that reason void (Article VI).

4. The decision allowed the growth of a national economy regulated by Congress and free from interference by state legislatures. Its effects included westward expansion of the country and the creation of national roads, canals, telegraphs, and railroads. It also allowed the Court to avoid enraging the southern states over slavery and slave trade.

Evaluation of the Case

1. Answers will vary but students should show they are aware of the constraints that local, state, or regional interests could impose. In discussion, suggest that instead of a national economy, the situation between states might have become as competitive as that between the United States and Japan or the EEC.

2. Answers should show that students understand that the attitudes of the Court do shift with political and social changes in the country.

3. Answers will vary, with some students thinking that the states might have successfully kept this power. Others might suggest that eventually some sort of central authority or agreement would have to evolve.

Extending the Lesson

1. A good video reenactment of the *Gibbons* case is included in the series "Equal Justice Under Law," funded by the Commission on the Bicentennial of the U.S. Constitution, chaired by Warren G. Burger. The video, *Gibbons v. Ogden,* is distributed by National Audio Visual Center, 8700 Edgeworth Drive, Capital Heights, Maryland, 20743-3701.

2. For firsthand experience with regulations on interstate commerce, have students visit a local radio or television station or satellite-dish dealer to learn about the federal regulations those businesses must follow.

Gibbons v. Ogden (1824)

Vocabulary

license   Official document authorizing the holder to perform certain actions. An "exclusive license" grants authority to only one person or organization.

monopoly   Situation in which a single individual or business controls an entire market, with little or no competition.

sue   To take formal, legal action against someone in a court of law.

forfeit   To be forced to give up something as a penalty or fine for breaking a law or rule.

jurisdiction   Legal right of a court to act in a particular case.

interstate commerce   Trade between people or businesses in different states; trade or business that crosses state lines.

Reviewing the Case

Aaron Ogden and Thomas Gibbons were competing steamship operators whose ships traveled the bays and rivers between New Jersey and New York City. Under a law passed in the New York legislature, Ogden had an "exclusive **license**," which in effect gave him the exclusive right to operate any vessel in those waters, if the vessel "be moved by means of fire or steam." The original owners of this **monopoly** were Robert Livingston and steamship designer Robert Fulton. An act passed in 1808 extended their exclusive right for a period not to exceed 30 years (that is, to 1838). They had transferred the license to John Livingston, who, in turn, had transferred it to Aaron Ogden.

Thomas Gibbons, a New Jersey resident, was operating his two ships, the *Stoudinger* and the *Bellona*, in the same waters. Ogden **sued** him in the trial court of New York and won. For Gibbons, this was a serious loss. The New York laws that gave Aaron Ogden exclusive navigation rights also provided that anyone violating the law would **forfeit** his ship. Gibbons therefore appealed the decision to the highest court in New York that had the **jurisdiction** to hear it. The appeal, like the original trial, ended in Ogden's favor. Gibbons was forbidden to operate his ships.

Gibbons was convinced that his right to navigate the waters between New York and New Jersey was clear and that his right had been taken from him unlawfully by the courts of New York. Before starting his business, Gibbons had obtained a license issued by the national government under the authority of a 1793 act of Congress. The license gave Gibbons the right to operate his ships in any coastal waters of the United States.

After losing in the state courts, Gibbons took his case to the United States Supreme Court. As Gibbons' attorney wrote in his statement to the Court, the process of the state courts had to be exhausted before the Supreme Court could act in the matter.

The battle between Gibbons and Ogden was not an isolated incident. Other states had passed similar laws, which had hampered the free exchange of goods from one state to another and caused resentment between neighbors in adjoining states.

The case clearly pointed up the conflict existing between laws passed by the legislature of the state of New York and the laws passed by the Congress of the United States. The issue before the Court: Do the laws passed by the New York legislature violate the Constitution of the United States by their attempt to regulate **interstate commerce** or are they permissible?

A further complication in the case was the strong feeling among southern states that to overturn the decision of the New York court in this case would destroy all state powers concerning commerce. This, the southern states concluded, would ultimately lead to a congressional right to eliminate the slave trade and eventually abolish slavery. There was a very real threat, then, that the South would feel obliged to resist such potential congressional power and withdraw from the Union.

Could the Court risk such a disastrous outcome or could it find some middle ground —one that would prevent state legislatures from passing laws that interfered with the free exchange of goods and services between the states but would also keep the South in the Union?

The answer was found in the Court's definition of *commerce*. Was commerce to be defined simply as the exchange of goods and services or did commerce also include the transportation of those goods and services to be exchanged? Chief Justice John Marshall stated:

The mind can scarcely conceive a system for regulating commerce between nations, which shall exclude all laws concerning navigation, which shall be silent on the admission of vessels of the one nation into the ports of the other, and be confined to prescribing rules for the conduct of individuals, in the actual employment of buying and selling, or of barter.

The Court then broadened the definition of the word *commerce* to include transportation, thereby allowing the regulation of transportation as it is involved in the exchange of goods and services. By broadening the definition of commerce, the Court declared the regulation of transportation to be clearly within the "commerce power" of Congress, as stated in Article 1, Section 8, Clause 3.

Does the power of Congress to regulate commerce extend into the territory of the various states? Yes, it does. As Justice Marshall wrote:

The power of Congress, then, comprehends navigation within the limits of every state in the Union; so far as that navigation may be, in manner, connected with [in the words of the Constitution] "commerce with foreign nations, or among the several states, or with the Indian tribes." It may, of consequence, pass the jurisdictional line of New York, and act upon the very waters to which the prohibition now under consideration applies.

The Constitution, the Court further pointed out, clearly states that national laws made in accordance with the Constitution are "the supreme law of the land," superior to conflicting state laws.

This decision placed the regulation of commerce across state boundaries clearly within the authority of the Congress. State laws that conflicted with this authority would not be permissible. That is, if an act of Congress gave Gibbons the right to sail on New York waters, a New York state law could not forbid him to do so. By settling the case in this way, the Court could keep the individual states from interfering in the conduct of trade by those living in other states. At the same time, the Court did not threaten the South by destroying all state powers concerning commerce. For the moment at least, the Court avoided a crisis over congressional interference in the slave trade.

The decision opened the door for the national government to pursue the expansion and growth of the national economy. By preventing state interference in the building of national roads, canals, and telegraph and railroad lines, the decision greatly enhanced the ability of the Congress to encourage and promote westward expansion and settlement.

Supreme Court Decision 4

Gibbons v. Ogden (1824)

Elements of the Case

Directions: Fill in the appropriate information for each of the following elements of this case.

1. State the issue before the Supreme Court in this case.

_____

_____

_____

_____

2. What facts of the case were presented to the Court?

_____

_____

_____

_____

3. What was the decision of the Court? What was the rationale behind it?

_____

_____

_____

4. What was the effect of the decision?

_____

_____

_____

_____

Evaluation of the Case

Directions: Use your own judgment to evaluate the justices' decision
and state your opinion about this case.

1. In your opinion, would the United States have grown into a major
    world power if it had not been able to establish a national economy,
    free from barriers imposed by individual state legislatures? Explain.

    _____

    _____

    _____

    _____

    _____

2. When deciding cases, should the Court concern itself with the possi-
    ble consequences, such as the threatened southern secession during
    this case? Explain.

    _____

    _____

    _____

    _____

    _____

3. Who would control the power to regulate commerce in the United
    States if this decision or a subsequent decision like it had not oc-
    curred? Explain.

    _____

    _____

    _____

    _____

    _____

Supreme Court Decision 5

Dartmouth College v. Woodward (1819)
Teacher Lesson Plan

Rationale

This lesson is designed to explore with students the growing role of the federal judiciary in the early 1800s. Under the leadership of Chief Justice John Marshall, the Supreme Court made a number of decisions that strengthened the new national government and the nation's sense of "nationalism." This Supreme Court case encouraged the growth of business by upholding the validity of contracts, as protected by the U.S. Constitution.

General Goals

This case study will provide students with opportunities to:

1. explore the challenges of American constitutional law
2. understand the processes and procedures of the judicial system
3. examine the role of the Supreme Court in the formation of public policy
4. explore the conflict between judicial activism and judicial restraint
5. examine the opinions of Supreme Court justices
6. demonstrate critical thinking skills

Directions

Student material is provided in four blackline masters on the following pages. These should be copied and distributed to students. They include a brief description of the *Dartmouth College* case as well as questions for students to answer.

Elements of the Case presents questions to check student comprehension, providing an opportunity to review with students the central issues, the Court's decision and rationale, and the effects of the case.

Evaluation of the Case provides one or more critical thinking activities for students. In this section, students are asked to evaluate the case and express their own positions on its issues.

Answer Key and Extending the Lesson

An answer key for the questions is provided on the next page, along with suggested activities for extending the lesson.

Dartmouth College v. Woodward

Answer Key

Elements of the Case

1. *Issue*: Did the acts of the state legislature, placing Dartmouth College under state control, violate the U.S. Constitution?
2. Dartmouth College had been chartered in 1769 by the king of England; control of the college had been given to its trustees. In 1816 the state of New Hampshire, regarding the school as public, passed a law to reorganize it as a state university. The college trustees sued on the grounds that the state had ignored the contract between them and the king, which was protected by the U.S. Constitution. The state supreme court upheld the legislature.
3. The Court ruled, with one dissent, that the New Hampshire legislature's action violated the constitutional ban of Article I, section 10 which stated: "no state . . . shall impair the legal obligation of a contract." It believed that the contract had survived the American Revolution, with the former responsibilities of the king passing to the new state government.
4. The Dartmouth College decision provided security in many institutions of the country. The decision was considered a positive step for the national economy and for all private corporations. It guaranteed the protection of all types of contracts from government actions.

    The decision was also significant because of John Marshall's classic definition of a "corporation."

Evaluation of the Case

1. Answers will vary, but students should understand that the framers, all men of property, were concerned with protecting property and other private interests from state governments, which were seen as popularly controlled.
2. Answers will vary; students who think that all contracts and existing arrangements should have started over should go on to question 3.
3. Answers will vary, with some students realizing that this would have caused considerable upheaval and instability, making it harder for the new American government to become established.

Extending the Lesson

1. John Marshall and Daniel Webster, both important participants in this case, had long careers and played extremely important roles in American history. Have one or two interested students investigate biographical information about these two men and report to the class.
2. Other colonial charters were also carried over into the new republic. Have students research how (1) state governments, (2) business organizations, or (3) private groups such as schools and charities used or kept their colonial charters in the years following the American Revolution.

Dartmouth College
v. Woodward (1824)

Vocabulary

charter A written document issued by a government or other authority, giving the holder the right to establish an organization such as a company or colony.

trustees Group of people named or elected to manage an organization, such as a college.

contract A legally binding agreement between two or more individuals or organizations.

dissent To disagree with the majority opinion of the majority of justices on the Court.

Reviewing the Case

In 1754, Eleazar Wheelock, an educator and popular preacher in colonial New England, established a school to teach Christianity and educate both white settlers and the local Native Americans. After inspiring success, Wheelock decided to expand. He solicited donations from people in England and was given a grant of land on the Connecticut River in western New Hampshire. He and other settlers, with about 30 students, founded a town and began Dartmouth College.

In 1769, Dartmouth College received a **charter** from King George III of England. The charter gave twelve **trustees** full power to govern the college, administer the funds, hire professors, direct the course of study, and fill vacancies in their ranks. The charter provided that the college corporation should always continue under twelve trustees.

In June 1816, the New Hampshire legislature passed an act to abandon the old charter, reorganize Dartmouth College, and make it a state-run university. It planned to add more trustees who would be appointed by the state governor. The legislature passed two additional acts later in the year to put the act into effect.

Most of the college trustees rebelled against this action. With the support of some professors and most of the students, they continued to operate privately. They then sued William Woodward, secretary-treasurer of the trustees who had joined the new school, to regain control of their corporate papers, the school seal, and other documents. The suit questioned whether the state law was constitutional.

New Hampshire's state supreme court ruled against Dartmouth College. It said that the school had changed, becoming public, and so belonged under state control. The question then went to the Supreme Court of the United States. The issue before the Court: Did the acts of the state legislature, placing Dartmouth College under state control, violate the U.S. Constitution?

Constitutionality was an issue because one goal of the framers of the U.S. Constitution was to protect private property from the state governments. For this reason, Article I, Section 10, includes what is known as the "**contract** clause." It specifically limits the actions of state governments: "No state shall . . . pass any . . . law impairing the obligation of contracts."

The Dartmouth College case was first argued before the Court in 1818 but was not decided until the following term. Daniel Webster, a well-known lawyer and orator who was a Dartmouth alumni, represented the college. Arguing for the school's rights, Webster said: "It is a small college and yet there are those who love it."

With one **dissenting** vote, the Court ruled that the legislature acted unlawfully when it took control of the college, violating Article I of the Constitution. Chief Justice John Marshall, who favored the college's point of view, wrote the opinion of the Court:

It can require no argument to prove that the circumstances of this case constitute a contract. An application is made to the crown [the English king] for a charter to incorporate a religious and literary institution. In the application, it is stated that large contributions have been made for the object, which will be conferred on the corporation soon as it shall be created. The charter is granted, and on its faith the property is conveyed. Surely in this transaction every ingredient of a complete contract is to be found. . . .

According to this decision, a corporate charter was considered to be a contract and so could not be broken by acts of a legislature. The Court noted that the American Revolution had simply shifted the duties and powers of government from the king to the people of New Hampshire. Property rights and contract rights had not been affected. Marshall added:

The obligations, then, which were created by the charter to Dartmouth College, were the same in the new [state government] that they had been in the old government.

Marshall found that the New Hampshire law destroyed the charter by taking the funds and control of the college from the trustees and giving them to the state government. He wrote:

The charter of 1769 exists no longer. It is reorganized; and reorganized in such a manner as to convert a literary institution, molded according to the will of its founders, and placed under the control of private literary men, into a machine entirely subservient to the will of government. This may be for the advantage of this college in particular . . . but it is not according to the will of the donors, and is subversive of that contract on the faith of which their property was given.

The Court reversed the state court's decision, ordered the documents returned to the trustees, and instructed the state to pay the trustees $20,000 in damages, along with legal fees and court costs.

The Dartmouth College case decision was considered a positive step for the national economy and for all private corporations. It guaranteed the protection of all types of contracts from government actions.

Also in this decision, Chief Justice Marshall gave a definition of a corporation that became a classic in law:

A corporation is an artificial being, invisible, intangible, and existing only in contemplation of law. Being the mere creature of law, it possesses only those properties which the charter of its creation confers upon it, either expressly or as incidental to its very existence. These [properties] are such as are supposed best calculated to effect the object for which it was created. Among the most important are immortality and . . . individuality.

Dartmouth College
v. Woodward (1824)

Elements of the Case

Directions: Fill in the appropriate information for each of the following elements of this case.

1. State the issue before the Supreme Court in this case.

_____

_____

_____

_____

_____

2. What facts of the case were presented to the Court?

_____

_____

_____

_____

_____

3. What was the decision of the Court? What was the rationale behind it?

_____

_____

_____

_____

4. What was the effect of the decision?

_____

_____

_____

_____

Evaluation of the Case

Directions: Use your own judgment to evaluate the justices' decision and state your opinion of that decision.

1. Why do you think the framers of the Constitution specifically denied state governments the right to interfere with legally-made contracts? Explain.

_____

_____

_____

_____

_____

2. In your opinion, should the American Revolution and the end of English rule have broken the contract made originally between the King and the trustees? Explain.

_____

_____

_____

_____

_____

3. What do you think the effect would have been on others who owned property, by way of a charter or contract, if the decision had gone against the trustees?

_____

_____

_____

_____

_____

Supreme Court Decision 6

Worcester v. Georgia (1832)
Teacher Lesson Plan

Rationale

This lesson is designed to explore with students the growing role of the federal judiciary in the early 1800s, particularly under the leadership of Chief Justice John Marshall. This Supreme Court case involved both the supremacy of national law and the rights of the Cherokee Nation, pitting the Court against the state of Georgia and other branches of the federal government.

General Goals

This case study will provide students with opportunities to:

1. explore the challenges of American constitutional law
2. understand the processes and procedures of the judicial system
3. examine the role of the Supreme Court in the formation of public policy
4. explore the conflict between judicial activism and judicial restraint
5. examine the opinions of Supreme Court justices
6. demonstrate critical thinking skills

Directions

Student material is provided in four blackline masters on the following pages. These should be copied and distributed to students. They include a brief description of the Cherokee Indian situation as well as questions for students to answer.

Elements of the Case presents questions to check student comprehension, providing an opportunity to review with students the central issues, the Court's decision and rationale, and the effects of the case.

Evaluation of the Case provides one or more critical thinking activities for students. In this section, students are asked to evaluate the case and express their own positions on its issues.

Answer Key and Extending the Lesson

An answer key for the questions is provided on the next page, along with suggested activities for extending the lesson.

Worcester v. Georgia (1832)

Answer Key

Elements of the Case

1. *Issue*: Are the Georgia statutes relating to the Cherokee Nation in violation of the Constitution of the United States?
2. The United States government had made several treaties with the Cherokee Nation that treated it as a sovereign power. The state of Georgia, however, passed laws taking jurisdiction over Cherokee lands, invalidating Cherokee laws, and making laws regarding the Cherokee territory. Samuel Worcester, a missionary, was arrested and convicted for defying one Georgia law, which made it illegal for a white person to live in Cherokee territory. He appealed his case to the Supreme Court as a test case, hoping the Court would affirm the Cherokee treaty rights and overturn the Georgia laws.
3. The Court upheld the validity of the Cherokee's treaty rights and said that Georgia laws were not valid in Cherokee territory. Only the national government had authority to deal with Indians; federal treaties and the Constitution took precedence over state laws. It also reversed the state court decision and ordered Worcester set free.
4. The Court decision upheld the supremacy of the Constitution and federal treaties, but President Jackson could and did ignore the affirmation of treaty rights and continued with his plans for Indian removal. Because the decision was not put into effect, the Native Americans of the Southeast were almost all forcibly moved to western lands in Oklahoma.

Evaluation of the Case

1. Answers should include the idea that, in order to uphold the Constitution, the Court had to rule against the policy of Indian removal that the administration and Congress were backing. Nevertheless, the Constitution says that not only the Constitution itself but also federal treaties are the supreme law of the land.
2. Answers will vary but should include the understanding that the Court has no enforcement powers.
3. Answers will vary, but students should realize that too many political forces were against the Cherokee; their lands were valuable to settlers.

Extending the Lesson

1. The Indian Removal Act of 1830, passed by Congress, was intended to remove all Indians to a location west of the Mississippi River. Ask students to speculate and discuss the changes in history that might have occurred if President Jackson had decided to enforce the Court's decision in this case and had respected the Cherokee Nation's right to remain and govern its own territory in Georgia.
2. Have students read and report on some of the accounts written on and about the "Trail of Tears."
3. The Cherokee people developed a written language with a syllabary and adopted a written constitution. Have interested students research the continuing culture of the Cherokee Nation, both in Oklahoma and in parts of the East.

Worcester v. Georgia (1832)

Vocabulary

sovereign Referring to a nation or government that has the right to rule itself and make its own laws.

writ of error An order from an appellate court to a lower court to send records of a case to the higher court to review for possible errors.

Reviewing the Case

After the War of 1812, official American government policy toward Native Americans in Eastern states focused on forcing the Indians off their native lands, which included some of the best farming land in the Southeast. One of the strongest advocates for removing the Indians from their lands was Andrew Jackson, elected President in 1828. By 1830 he had persuaded Congress to pass the Indian Removal Act, which ordered the forced relocation of all the Indians of the Southeast. One large group was the Cherokee Nation, who tried to use the federal courts to defend themselves.

The United States government had earlier made treaties with the Cherokee Nation in Georgia, treating them as a **sovereign** people. These treaties were supposed to secure the Indian lands. Later, the federal government withdrew some of its support for Indian land claims. In 1824 Georgia claimed jurisdiction over all the Cherokee lands in the state. The Cherokee then adopted their own written constitution and claimed independence within the state. Georgia in turn passed new laws that denied all Indian land claims and put the territories under state law. The state also claimed that the federal government's treaties had no authority in the state.

President Jackson supported the state against the Indians. Congress urged a compromise or voluntary resettlement. The Cherokee tried to bring one case to the Supreme Court on the grounds that they were a foreign nation, but political opposition made this attempt fail.

In 1832 Samuel Worcester, a missionary, deliberately defied a Georgia statute that prohibited any white person from entering Cherokee territory without taking an oath of allegiance as prescribed by Georgia law and obtaining a license signed by the governor. Worcester was living among the Cherokee Indians within Gwinnett County. Like other missionaries who defied the law, he hoped to test the Georgia anti-Cherokee laws in the Supreme Court.

Worcester was indicted, arrested, and convicted by a jury of the Superior Court of Gwinnett County. He and another missionary were sentenced to four years of hard labor. Worcester asked the United States Supreme Court for a **writ of error**, and Chief Justice John Marshall agreed to review the case.

The state of Georgia in turn refused to appear because it said the Court was unlawfully taking away state powers. Even before the case was heard, the state legislature passed laws giving the governor authority to use force to resist any attempt to overturn state laws.

Worcester's case alleged that the state of Georgia had no authority in the Cherokee territory despite the fact it existed within the territorial boundaries of that state. Worcester also stated that various treaties by the United States government recognized the Cherokee as a sovereign nation, meaning that Congress was the only legislative body with the authority to deal with them.

The *Worcester* case was now a power struggle involving the Supreme Court, the President, the state of Georgia, and the Constitution. The issue before the Court: Are the Georgia statutes relating to the Cherokee Nation in violation of the Constitution of the United States?

The Court with one dissenting vote upheld the Cherokees' treaty rights in Georgia. Chief

Justice Marshall supported the authority of the Cherokee within their treaty boundaries where, he said, the laws of Georgia were not in effect. The Georgia statutes to the contrary were not constitutional; they were "repugnant to the Constitution, laws, and treaties of the United States." Only the United States government had authority in Indian affairs. The Court also reversed the state court's decision and ordered that Worcester be freed.

In his opinion, Chief Justice Marshall explained the ruling:

It has been shown that the treaties and laws referred to come within the due exercise of the constitutional powers of the federal government; that they may remain in full force, and consequently must be considered then as the supreme law of the land. These laws throw a shield over the Cherokee Indian. They guarantee to them their rights of occupancy, of self-government, and the full enjoyment of the blessings which might be attained in their humble condition. . . .

Other justices also agreed that only the national government, not any individual state, had the authority to make laws affecting the Cherokee Nation.

While defending the Constitution as the supreme law of the land, the Court had enraged the state of Georgia and contradicted the President's desire to move the Indians of the Southeast. It seemed unlikely that President Jackson would do anything to support the Court's decisions. Supposedly, Jackson responded to the decision by saying, "John Marshall has made his decision; now let him enforce it." Eventually, however, political considerations led Jackson to persuade the governor of Georgia to free Worcester.

Despite the Supreme Court's affirmation of their treaty rights, the Cherokee could not win in the long run. Jackson did nothing to enforce the Court's decision regarding the Native Americans' rights. A few years later, in 1838 and 1839, nearly all the Cherokee, along with other Southeastern Indians, were forcibly moved westward on "the Trail of Tears."

Name _____ Date _____

Worcester v. Georgia (1832)

Elements of the Case

Directions: Fill in the appropriate information for each of the following elements of this case.

1. State the issue before the Supreme Court in this case.

_____

_____

_____

_____

2. What facts of the case were presented to the Court?

_____

_____

_____

_____

3. What was the decision of the Court? What was the rationale behind it?

_____

_____

_____

4. What was the effect of the decision?

_____

_____

_____

_____

Supreme Court Decision 6

Evaluation of the Case

Directions: Use your own judgment to evaluate the justices' decision and state your opinion of that decision.

1. Why was this Court decision important in maintaining the supremacy of the Constitution? What was dangerous about the decision?

_____

_____

_____

_____

_____

2. What did President Jackson's remark and his refusal to enforce the decision reveal about the separation of powers established in the Constitution? Can the Court enforce its decisions without executive cooperation? Explain.

_____

_____

_____

_____

_____

3. Do you think that, at this point in history, anything could have been done to save the Cherokee Nation's lands in the Southeast? Explain why or why not.

_____

_____

_____

_____

_____

Supreme Court Decision 7

United States v. E.C. Knight (1895)
Teacher Lesson Plan

Rationale

This lesson is designed to explore with students the struggles during the 1890s between Populists and other reformers and the entrenched "establishment" of bankers, business leaders, and many politicians. This Supreme Court case was an unsuccessful attempt to apply the provisions of the recent Sherman Antitrust Act (1890) to a monopoly in the sugar industry.

General Goals

This case study will provide students with opportunities to:

1. explore the challenges of American constitutional law
2. understand the processes and procedures of the judicial system
3. examine the role of the Supreme Court in the formation of public policy
4. explore the conflict between judicial activism and judicial restraint
5. examine the opinions of Supreme Court justices
6. demonstrate critical thinking skills

Directions

Student material is provided in four blackline masters on the following pages. These should be copied and distributed to students. They include a brief description of the *E. C. Knight* case as well as questions for students to answer.

Elements of the Case presents questions to check student comprehension, providing an opportunity to review with students the central issues, the Court's decision and rationale, and the effects of the case.

Evaluation of the Case provides one or more critical thinking activities for students. In this section, students are asked to evaluate the case and express their own positions on its issues.

Answer Key and Extending the Lesson

An answer key for the questions is provided on the next page, along with suggested activities for extending the lesson.

United States v. E. C. Knight (1895)

Answer Key

Elements of the Case

1. *Issue:* Do the contracts between American Sugar Refining Company and four other sugar refiners create an unlawful monopoly that violates the Sherman Antitrust Act?

2. American Sugar Refining Company, the "Sugar Trust," made contracts to buy four other refiners, which would have given one company control of 98% of the sugar refining industry in the United States. The federal government sued to stop the transactions under the Sherman Antitrust Act of 1890, which was meant to control combinations in restraint of trade.

3. The Court ruled 8–1 that the Sherman Act did not apply. It said that the sugar refineries were all within one state, taking the issue out of "interstate commerce," even though the products would be sold in other states. The Court also made a distinction between manufacturing and commerce, stating that a monopoly in manufacturing did not necessarily mean an intent to monopolize sales.

4. The decision effectively exempted manufacturing from federal regulations regarding monopolies. This allowed the growth and merger of many companies. Businesses unfairly took advantage of this decision to combine and fix prices. The decision severely weakened the Sherman Antitrust Act. Populists, reformers, and ordinary people were further convinced that the government would always side with the rich and with big business.

Evaluation of the Case

1. Answers will vary, but many students may find Justice Fuller's opinion too narrow and hairsplitting.

2. Answers should show that students understand the abuses of trusts and monopolies or near-monopolies in the 1890s and early 1900s, as well as the potential for any monopoly to control prices, quality, supply, etc.

3. Answers will vary depending on students' economic knowledge and philosophies.

Extending the Lesson

1. Ask students to apply the Knight decision to contemporary situations. Have them discuss what the consequences would be if the federal government could not regulate (1) oil companies, (2) coal companies, or (3) utilities/energy companies.

2. The 1980s and 1990s saw an increase in mergers in a number of industries, including banking and communications. Have students use the *Readers' Guide* or other library periodicals index to compile a list of some of these large mergers. Then have small groups research several of the significant mergers (e.g., Time-Warner) and report on the companies involved and the potential consequences for that industry and for the economy as a whole.

United States v. E. C. Knight (1895)

Vocabulary

monopoly Situation in which a single individual or business controls an entire market, with little or no competition.

trust Group of companies whose stock is controlled by a central board of directors.

Reviewing the Case

The Sherman Antitrust Act was passed in 1890 as an attempt to control the growth of big business and prevent the development of **monopolies.** Enforcing the act, however, was a severe problem. One of the difficulties was the tendency of the courts to favor big business, made worse by the vagueness of the wording in the act itself. This Supreme Court decision marked one early failure of the Sherman Act.

In March 1892, the American Sugar Refining Company, which already dominated the industry, made contracts to purchase the E. C. Knight Company and three other sugar manufacturing companies in Philadelphia, Pennsylvania. These companies included all but one of the sugar refining firms in the United States and were the only competition faced by the American Sugar Refining Company, which was known as the "Sugar Trust." The four companies to be purchased would exchange their own stock for American Sugar Refining stock. With this transaction, the combined holdings of the company would amount to 98 percent of all sugar processing in the United States.

The federal government charged, under the Sherman Antitrust Act, that the transactions would give American Sugar Refining Company control of sugar prices along with a monopoly on manufacturing and selling refined sugar. The government alleged that controlling the manufacture of sugar also involved interstate commerce, since people everywhere in the country needed and would buy sugar. It believed that the goal of this business transaction was to control the sugar market.

After losing its case in the circuit court and the U.S. Circuit Court of Appeals, the government took the case to the U.S. Supreme Court. The issue before the Court: Do the contracts between American Sugar Refining Company and the four other companies create an unlawful monopoly that violates the Sherman Antitrust Act?

Interpreting the Sherman Act very narrowly, the Supreme Court voted 8-1 that the act could not be applied in this case. As the Court restated the Sherman Act, its purpose was to prohibit conspiracies or combinations that were intended to restrain commerce between the states or with foreign countries. It did not feel that acquiring sugar refineries in the state of Pennsylvania directly affected interstate commerce.

The Court made a distinction between *manufacturing* sugar and *selling* sugar. It said that even if the trust had a monopoly in manufacturing, it was not necessarily trying to monopolize commerce. The effects on trade were indirect effects, so that this transaction did not come under the Sherman Antitrust Act—or under the constitutional powers of Congress to regulate commerce.

Chief Justice Melville Fuller wrote for the Court majority:

> . . . Commerce succeeds to manufacture and is not a part of it. The power to regulate commerce is the power to prescribe the rule by which commerce shall be governed, and is a power independent of the power to suppress monopoly. . . .
>
> . . . The fact that an article is manufactured for export to another State does not of itself make it an article of interstate commerce, and the intent of the manufacturer does not determine the time when the article or product passes from the control of the State and belongs to commerce. . . .

Justice John Marshall Harlan, the only dissenting justice, felt that this interpretation was so narrow and rigid that it prevented the national government from carrying out its authority over commerce. "While the opinion of the Court in this case," Harlan said, "does not declare the Act of 1890 to be unconstitutional, it defeats the main object for which it was passed."

Harlan also did not accept Justice Fuller's distinction between manufacturing and selling, since sales throughout the country were clearly the goal of the Sugar Trust. For Harlan, the issue was not the contracts but the trust's control over sales of sugar. His dissent said, in part:

> The end proposed to be accomplished by the act of 1890 [the Sherman Act] is the protection of trade and commerce among the States against unlawful restraints. Who can say that that end is not legitimate or is not within the scope of the Constitution? The means employed are the suppression, by legal proceedings, of combinations, conspiracies, and monopolies, which by their inevitable and admitted tendency, improperly restrain trade and commerce among the States. . . . What clause of the Constitution can be referred to which prohibits the means thus prescribed in the Act of Congress?

The *E. C. Knight* decision, like others of the period, reflected the Court's reluctance to interfere with big business. It provided evidence for the Populists and other reformers that the Court was on the side of the rich.

The decision essentially exempted manufacturing companies from the Sherman Antitrust Act. In the decades following the decision, many mergers and combinations took place to create massive concentrations of power in a few giant corporations. Corporate giants such as U.S. Steel, International Harvester, and Standard Oil of New Jersey benefited from the decision.

Name _____ Date _____

United States v. E. C. Knight (1895)

Elements of the Case

Directions: Fill in the appropriate information for each of the following elements of this case.

1. State the issue before the Supreme Court in this case.

_____

_____

_____

_____

2. What facts of the case were presented to the Court?

_____

_____

_____

_____

3. What was the decision of the Court? What was the rationale behind it?

_____

_____

_____

4. What was the effect of the decision?

_____

_____

_____

_____

Supreme Court Decision 7

Evaluation of the Case

Directions: Use your own judgment to evaluate the justices' decision and state your opinion of that decision.

1. With which opinion did you agree in this case—the majority or Justice Harlan's dissent?

_____

_____

_____

_____

_____

2. Why do you think did Congress try to regulate monopolies and trusts? What is wrong with one or a few companies controlling an entire industry?

_____

_____

_____

_____

_____

3. What are the advantages of federal regulations applying to businesses throughout the country? What limits do you think should be placed on them? Where, do you think, should federal regulation give way to state regulation? Explain.

_____

_____

_____

_____

_____

Supreme Court Decision 8

Pollock v. Farmers Loan & Trust Co. (1895)
Teacher Lesson Plan

Rationale

This lesson is designed to explore with students the movements for change and reform that took place in the 1890s and early 1900s, led by Populists and Progressives. This Supreme Court case marked the defeat of one of the first efforts to impose an income tax, an issue that some people considered a direct attack on capitalism and business.

General Goals

This case study will provide students with opportunities to:

1. explore the challenges of American constitutional law
2. understand the processes and procedures of the judicial system
3. examine the role of the Supreme Court in the formation of public policy
4. explore the conflict between judicial activism and judicial restraint
5. examine the opinions of Supreme Court justices
6. demonstrate critical thinking skills

Directions

Student material is provided in four blackline masters on the following pages. These should be copied and distributed to students. They include a brief description of the *Pollock* case as well as questions for students to answer.

Elements of the Case presents questions to check student comprehension, providing an opportunity to review with students the central issues, the Court's decision and rationale, and the effects of the case.

Evaluation of the Case provides one or more critical thinking activities for students. In this section, students are asked to evaluate the case and express their own positions on its issues.

Answer Key and Extending the Lesson

An answer key for the questions is provided on the next page, along with suggested activities for extending the lesson.

Pollock v. Farmers Loan & Trust Co.
(1895)

Answer Key

Elements of the Case

1. *Issue:* Is the income tax provision of the Wilson-Gorman Tariff passed by Congress in 1894 a direct tax in violation of the Constitution?
2. An 1894 tariff bill included an income tax on incomes above $4,000, including income from property and investments. The Farmers' Loan & Trust Company, to comply, intended to pay the 2% tax on its investors' incomes from real estate and New York City municipal bonds. A group headed by Pollock sued to prevent this payment on the grounds that the income tax violated the constitutional provisions regarding direct taxes.
3. The Court split on many parts of the tax but voted in favor of Pollock that taxes on the *income* from real estate and investments were like taxes on the property itself. They would therefore amount to direct taxes, which were unconstitutional. Taxes on income from municipal bonds were not allowed because they interfered with a state power. The Court would have allowed an income tax on wages and salaries, but the whole law was overturned.
4. The decision was a clear victory for the wealthy and a setback for the Populists' attempts to shift the burden of taxes to the wealthy. Imbalances in income grew worse until the passage of the Sixteenth Amendment, allowing the income tax.

Evaluation of the Case

1. Answers will vary, though many students may agree with the dissenting justices as to the decision's unfairness, or they may think that parts of the decision are fair and parts are not.
2. Students should understand that taxing the income from such bonds would probably make it more difficult for cities to fund public works projects, as these bonds may not pay as well as corporate bonds.
3. Answers will vary, but students should show they understand the hairsplitting distinction the Court made in order to protect property and investment income.

Extending the Lesson

1. Can different governments tax each other's institutions, financial instruments (such as bonds), and the like? This question also arose in *McCulloch v. Maryland.* Have students investigate state and federal tax laws and consider what they find in terms of John Marshall's statement that "The power to tax is the power to destroy."
2. *Pollock* is one of a few Supreme Court decisions that was changed by later constitutional amendment. The others are *Chisholm v. Georgia*, Eleventh Amendment; and *Dred Scott v. Sanford* (Decision 11 in this book), Fourteenth Amendment. Have students discuss how such changes show that the Supreme Court often encounters issues just as they are becoming part of the public's consciousness.

Pollock v. Farmers Loan & Trust Co. (1895)

Vocabulary

tariff A tax on imported or exported products.

municipal bonds Bonds sold by cities to raise money for projects such as improving public transportation or constructing new public buildings.

Reviewing the Case

Although the Constitution originally gave Congress the power to impose taxes, it also set certain limits on direct taxes. The constitution says that these must be apportioned, or divided, among the states according to population. Over the years, various court decisions established that direct taxes were those imposed on people (poll taxes) or on property. Although the federal government today collects income taxes, it could not do so legally for many years. This case was one step in the process.

During the 1880s and 1890s, the gap between the "haves" and the "have nots" in America increased. The Populists, speaking for working-class people, worked for reforms in government and controls on the economy. To achieve economic fairness, Populists believed that the wealthy should pay a greater share of the money needed to operate the government. At the time, most government income came from **tariffs** and excise taxes, paid by consumers. The Populists supported the idea of an income tax, believing it was fairer.

The Wilson-Gorman Tariff of 1894 was intended to lower import tariffs. Manufacturers, however, favored high tariffs, which raised the prices of imported goods and supposedly made American-made products more attractive to buyers. Siding with business interests, Congress made so many changes and additions in the tariff bill that tariffs remained high.

One section of the tariff bill, however, imposed an income tax of 2 percent on all annual incomes over $4,000. (Average annual income per person at the time was less than $400.) Income included interest from investments, such as stocks and bonds, as well as the income and rents from real estate—land and property. Since the wealthy owned more land and property and had more money to invest, the tax would affect them most—and they fought it in the courts.

To comply with the new tax law, the Farmers' Loan & Trust Company had to pay the 2 percent income tax on the profits of the property and investments it held for its investors. A group of those stockholders, headed by Charles Pollock of Massachusetts, brought suit to stop the bank from paying the tax. They charged that the tax was unconstitutional in two ways: It was a direct tax imposed without considering population, and it was imposed on the New York City **municipal bonds** held by the trust company.

The U.S. Circuit Court ruled in favor of the trust company, and the case came before the United States Supreme Court on appeal. The issue before the Court: Is the income tax provision of the Wilson-Gorman Tariff a direct tax in violation of the Constitution?

The Supreme Court heard the case twice and voted separately on a number of issues. Lawyers opposing the income tax attacked it as "socialistic" and "communistic," warning that it would destroy capitalism. The final 5-4 decision against the tax was seen as a complete victory for wealthy property owners whose incomes came mainly from investments.

The Court majority reasoned that a tax on the *income* from land was the same as a tax on the land itself. Since property taxes were direct taxes, said the Court, a tax on the income was also a direct tax. Similarly, the tax on income from investment property was a direct tax. Both were unconstitutional.

Chief Justice Melville Fuller summarized the majority opinion:

> *First.* We adhere to the opinion already announced, that, taxes on real estate being indisputably direct taxes, taxes on the rents or incomes of real estate are equally direct taxes.
>
> *Second.* We are of opinion that taxes on personal property, or on the income of personal property, are likewise direct taxes.

On the question of taxing municipal bonds, the Court ruled that Congress could not do so because it would interfere with the power of states to allow municipal governments to raise revenues through borrowing.

The dissents to the opinion in *Pollock* were angry and emotional. Justice John Marshall Harlan disagreed with the idea that taxing the income from land was the same as taxing land. He accused the majority justices of using the Court's power arbitrarily on behalf of private wealth. Another dissenting justice, Henry B. Brown, called the decision "a surrender of the taxing power to the moneyed class." He thought the majority were voting against the tax simply because they disliked the idea, not because the legal arguments against it were valid.

The Court did not find all parts of the tax law unconstitutional, although the law as a whole was struck down. But the dissenting justices pointed out that the provisions that the Court was willing to let stand were taxes on incomes from wages and salaries, while it rejected taxes on land and investments. Even if Congress reenacted this part of the bill, it would place all the tax burden on ordinary workers and wage earners, not on people with large estates and investments.

Public opinion opposed the *Pollock* decision, but some Republican newspapers saw it as timely opposition to the dangerous threats of populism and reform. One newspaper said that the Supreme Court had stopped a "communist revolution."

On the other hand, the decision encouraged proposals in the Democratic Party for a constitutional amendment. In the meantime, income imbalances between rich and poor continued to increase. It was not until 1913, with the ratification of the Sixteenth Amendment, that the income tax become constitutional.

Name _____   Date _____

Pollock v. Farmers Loan & Trust Co.
(1895)

Elements of the Case

Directions: Fill in the appropriate information for each of the following elements of this case.

1. State the issue before the Supreme Court in this case.

_____

_____

_____

_____

_____

2. What facts of the case were presented to the Court?

_____

_____

_____

_____

_____

3. What was the decision of the Court? What was the rationale behind it?

_____

_____

_____

_____

4. What was the effect of the decision?

_____

_____

_____

_____

Name _____ *Pollock v. Farmers Loan & Trust Co.* (cont.)

Evaluation of the Case

Directions: Use your own judgment to evaluate the justices' decision
and state your opinion of that decision.

1. Do you agree with the decision of the Court in this case? Explain.

_____

_____

_____

_____

2. Discuss the effect upon the states and cities to fund public projects
    (roads, bridges, schools, sports facilities) if the national government
    were allowed to tax the income from municipal bonds. Explain.

_____

_____

_____

_____

3. The Court in this case did not allow a tax on income from land or in-
    vestments, but it would have allowed a tax on income earned as
    wages or salaries. Do you think this decision was reasonable or fair?
    Explain your opinion.

_____

_____

_____

_____

Supreme Court Decision 8

Supreme Court Decision 9

Holden v. Hardy (1898)
Teacher Lesson Plan

Rationale

This lesson is designed to explore with students the changing attitudes toward social and economic legislation that were part of the Progressive era. This Supreme Court case marked the first time in which the Court accepted the constitutionality of a law regulating working conditions.

General Goals

This case study will provide students with opportunities to:

1. explore the challenges of American constitutional law
2. understand the processes and procedures of the judicial system
3. examine the role of the Supreme Court in the formation of public policy
4. explore the conflict between judicial activism and judicial restraint
5. examine the opinions of Supreme Court justices
6. demonstrate critical thinking skills

Directions

Student material is provided in four blackline masters on the following pages. These should be copied and distributed to students. They include a brief description of the *Holden* case as well as questions for students to answer.

Elements of the Case presents questions to check student comprehension, providing an opportunity to review with students the central issues, the Court's decision and rationale, and the effects of the case.

Evaluation of the Case provides one or more critical thinking activities for students. In this section, students are asked to evaluate the case and express their own positions on its issues.

Answer Key and Extending the Lesson

An answer key for the questions is provided on the next page, along with suggested activities for extending the lesson.

Holden v. Hardy (1898)

Answer Key

Elements of the Case

1. *Issue:* Does the Utah statute regulating working hours in the mining industry violate the rights of Holden, a U.S. citizen, under the Fourteenth Amendment?
2. An 1896 Utah law limited working hours in the mining industry to eight hours a day. Holden, a mining company owner, admitted that he had hired two men under contracts requiring them to work 10 and 12 hours a day respectively. He pled not guilty because he believed the law violated the Fourteenth Amendment in several ways: the right of employers (himself) and employees freely to make work contracts; his "privileges and immunities" as a citizen; and his loss of liberty and property without due process. The Utah constitution, however, provided protection for workers; the legislature considered the law a use of the state's police power. The state supreme court agreed.
3. The Supreme Court upheld the Utah law and affirmed the decision of the state courts. The justices believed the law was within the legitimate powers of the state to protect its citizens who worked in this dangerous industry.
4. The decision marked the first time such a law limiting business practices had been declared by the Court to be constitutional. The justices also acknowledged that the liberty of contract had limits. The decision encouraged progressive legislators in other states to pass similar protective legislation.

Evaluation of the Case

1. Most students will agree with Justice Brown that, in most cases, the employee has much less power than the company to negotiate a contract that protects his or her interests. The assumption about "liberty of contract" was made mainly by employers.
2. Answers may vary, but most students today will accept the principle that the state can set such regulations for all businesses.
3. Answers will vary, but this was the first successful Court test of progressive legislation governing working conditions. It made other legislation possible.
4. Answers will vary, although most students will agree that young children should not work in mining. Some may question the prohibition of women, who now work widely in jobs once thought too harsh or dangerous.

Extending the Lesson

1. Have students read and report on any one of the following books by "muckraker" writers concerning working conditions and safety abuses in the late nineteenth and early twentieth centuries: *The Jungle,* by Upton Sinclair (1906), *The Woman Who Toils,* by Mary and Bessy Van Vorst (1903), *How the Other Half Lives,* by Jacob Riis (1890), *The Shame of the Cities,* by Lincoln Steffens (1904), *The Bitter Cry of the Children,* by John Spargo (1906).
2. Have students research what kinds of laws your state has regarding hours of work, ages of workers, and similar circumstances. If possible, have them research when such laws were first passed in your state. Were they challenged by employers at the time?

Holden v. Hardy (1898)

Vocabulary

due process of law The constitutional right of every citizen to fair treatment under the law, including specific legal processes. Due process is protected by both the Fifth Amendment (federal government) and the Fourteenth Amendment (state government).

affirm To agree or support, as when a higher court (such as the Supreme Court) sustains the decision of a lower court (a state court or District Court).

Reviewing the Case

Government regulation of business in any way—even to protect the health and safety of workers—was an idea that met great resistance in the late 19th-century United States. Courts generally favored the property rights of employers over the rights of employees. A popular attitude was the idea of liberty of contract—the doctrine that employers and employees could both freely make a contract about work, with which the state could not interfere. This doctrine was popular with business interests and was the basis for many pro-business laws and court decisions at the time.

The *Hardy* case began when the Utah legislature recognized the hazards of the mining industry in the state. In March 1896, it passed a law providing a maximum eight-hour working day for miners and workers in smelters, the factories that process and refine metal ores.

A few months later, Albert Holden, a mining company owner, was arrested in Salt Lake City, Utah, and charged with breaking this law. He was charged specifically with entering into and executing unlawful contracts with two men. One of the men was required to work 10 hours a day in the underground mines owned by the company. The other was required by contract to work 12 hours a day in a factory that reduced and refined metal ores.

Before the Justice of the Peace, Albert Holden verified that the facts of the charges were accurate. He stated, however, that he was innocent on the grounds that the law under which the charges were made violated his constitutional rights. Found guilty, he was fined $50 and sentenced to 15 days in jail until the fine was paid. Holden, representing the mining company, applied to the Utah Supreme Court to reverse the decision.

The state court refused the application after reviewing the law in relation to the state constitution of Utah. One article of the state constitution was devoted entirely to the specific rights of labor. Using this part of the constitution as its standard, the Utah Supreme Court denied Holden's application and placed him in the custody of the sheriff, Harvey Hardy.

Holden appealed the case to the United States Supreme Court. He repeated the argument made before the Utah Supreme Court. First, he charged that the Utah legislature had no right to pass laws such as the one he was accused of violating. He stated that the law deprived both employers and employees of equal protection of the laws, guaranteed by the Fourteenth Amendment. It violated the principle of liberty of contract. Holden also said that the law abridged the "privileges and immunities" guaranteed to him as a citizen of the United States and deprived him of his property and liberty without **due process of law**.

The issue before the Court: Does the Utah statute regulating work hours in the mining industry violate the rights of Holden, a U.S. citizen, under the Fourteenth Amendment?

The Supreme Court voted 7–2 to uphold the Utah statute limiting working hours and to **affirm** the decision of the Utah Supreme Court. Justice Henry Billings Brown, writing the majority opinion of the Court, stated:

We are of the opinion that the Act in question was a valid exercise of the police powers of the state, and the judgments of the Supreme Court of Utah are therefore confirmed.

Although Justice Brown was not known for his liberal views, he did in this case point out that, despite the doctrine of liberty of contract, workers had much less bargaining power than employers in making contracts about jobs. Therefore, it was reasonable for the state to even out the balance.

This decision did not mean that the justices necessarily favored workers over employers or were giving up the idea of liberty of contract. The majority did acknowledge, however, that this liberty could be limited by the state's need to protect its citizens' health and lives. In this case, the Utah legislature assumed that mining was dangerous work and that excessively long work days in underground mines and in smelters or mills made it even more hazardous, contributing to accidents and deaths on the job. The justices could view the law as a health measure, not a labor law.

The *Holden v. Hardy* decision was a milestone—the first Court approval of a law limiting working hours. Progressive legislators in other states could also pass laws to protect their workers' safety by prohibiting company contracts that exceeded eight hours a day, thus protecting workers from threats of dismissal for refusing to work ten or more hours per day.

Business owners would continue to challenge these progressive laws over the next several decades, and many would be rejected. Nevertheless, despite its limits, this case was a tremendous victory for labor.

Name _____   Date _____

Holden v. Hardy (1898)

Elements of the Case

Directions: Fill in the appropriate information for each of the following elements of this case.

1. State the issue before the Supreme Court in this case.

_____

_____

_____

_____

_____

2. What facts of the case were presented to the Court?

_____

_____

_____

_____

_____

3. What was the decision of the Court? What was the rationale behind it?

_____

_____

_____

_____

4. What was the effect of the decision?

_____

_____

_____

_____

Supreme Court Decision 9

Evaluation of the Case

Directions: Use your own judgment to evaluate the justices' decision and state your opinion of that decision.

1. What is your reaction to the doctrine of liberty of contract when it applies to employers and employees? Should the state be able to interfere in a contract between two individuals if both are of legal age? Explain.

_____

_____

_____

_____

2. The Utah law applied only to workers in mining. Do you think such state legislation limiting working hours should apply only to dangerous work? Why or why not?

_____

_____

_____

_____

3. Why did Progressives consider this decision to be a victory? Was it? Explain.

_____

_____

_____

_____

4. Although it was not an issue in this case, the Utah constitution prohibited mining companies from employing women or children under age 14 in underground mines. Evaluate this provision of the law. Would you support it? Explain.

_____

_____

_____

_____

Supreme Court Decision 10

Lochner v. New York (1905)
Teacher Lesson Plan

Rationale

This lesson is designed to explore with students the changes in government attitudes toward business regulation that came about in the early 1900s as a result of the Progressive Movement. This Supreme Court decision, now regarded as a "museum piece," established the doctrine that the state could not usually interfere between employer and employee to regulate hours and wages.

General Goals

This case study will provide students with opportunities to:

1. explore the challenges of American constitutional law
2. understand the processes and procedures of the judicial system
3. examine the role of the Supreme Court in the formation of public policy
4. explore the conflict between judicial activism and judicial restraint
5. examine the opinions of Supreme Court justices
6. demonstrate critical thinking skills

Directions

Student material is provided in four blackline masters on the following pages. These should be copied and distributed to students. They include a brief description of the *Lochner* case as well as questions for students to answer.

Elements of the Case presents questions to check student comprehension, providing an opportunity to review with students the central issues, the Court's decision and rationale, and the effects of the case.

Evaluation of the Case provides one or more critical thinking activities for students. In this section, students are asked to evaluate the case and express their own positions on its issues.

Answer Key and Extending the Lesson

An answer key for the questions is provided on the next page, along with suggested activities for extending the lesson.

Lochner v. New York (1905)

Answer Key

Elements of the Case

1. *Issue*: Does the New York Labor Law unnecessarily interfere with the freedom to contract for labor in the bakery business?
2. New York State passed a law regulating working hours in the baking industry, limiting an individual to a maximum of 10 hours a day and 60 hours a week. Joseph Lochner, a bakery owner, was twice arrested for violating the law. He defended his actions on the grounds that the state law violated his right to contract under the Fourteenth Amendment.
3. The Supreme Court narrowly overturned the decision of the state courts and supported Lochner. The majority agreed that the Labor Law was in violation of the Fourteenth Amendment, interfering with the idea of liberty of contract between employer and employee. They did not think that baking was a hazardous enough job to warrant an exception on health grounds.
4. The *Lochner* decision was a setback for progressive legislation and the trend toward allowing states to use their powers in regulating working conditions and protecting workers. The dissents by both Harlan and Holmes would affect future decisions.

Evaluation of the Case

1. Answers will vary, depending in part on students' own work experience. Some may think that people should have the right to put in as much time as they want; point out that these contracts made no provision for "overtime" or extra pay for extra hours.
2. Answers will vary; in Justice Harlan's dissent, he believed that state legislators were closer to the situation and could investigate it better.
3. Answers should show that students grasp the basic idea that this doctrine regarded an individual employee and a corporation or company as equal bargainers in developing a contract (real or implied) regarding wages, hours, etc. For most ordinary workers, this was not a reality.

Extending the Lesson

1. What were working conditions and hours like in the early 1900s for ordinary workers in industries such as bakeries, food processing, and the garment industry? Have students investigate and report on what the lives of these workers were like. Good sources include the following books by "muckraking" authors: *The Jungle,* by Upton Sinclair (1906); *The Woman Who Toils*, by Mary and Bessy Van Vorst (1903); *How the Other Half Lives,* by Jacob Riis (1890); *The Shame of the Cities,* by Lincoln Steffens (1904); *The Bitter Cry of the Children,* by John Spargo (1906).
2. Have some students write to a New York newspaper and request a photocopy from their archives of a news story or editorial concerning this case. Some libraries may also have *Readers' Guide* listings to periodicals and magazines available on microfilm. Have students report on their findings, giving the case in the perspective of journalists of the time.

Lochner v. New York (1905)

Vocabulary

laissez faire Theory that government should not interfere in economic or business affairs (from French "allow to do").

Reviewing the Case

Progressive and reform legislators in the late 1800s and early 1900s made many changes in government and passed numerous laws trying to protect public health and safety. Some of the most controversial involved regulating businesses—working conditions, number of hours worked, and laws against child labor. When businesses challenged such laws in court, it was often under the concept of liberty of contract. This theory assumed that employers and prospective workers were both free individuals who could bargain on equal terms regarding wages, hours, and working conditions. A state legislature could not interfere with this implied contract, which was protected by the Fourteenth Amendment.

In 1897, the New York state legislature passed a statute known as the Labor Law. It applied to workers in any "biscuit, bread or cake bakery or confectionery establishment," limiting their working hours to no more than 60 in a week or more than 10 hours in any one day. After investigating conditions in the baking industry, state legislators had felt the new law was necessary to protect workers' health.

Joseph Lochner, a bakery owner, was twice arrested and convicted in the County Court of Oneida, New York, for breaking this law. On his second conviction, he was fined $50 and sent to jail until the fine was paid. He appealed, but the state supreme court affirmed the ruling. The case then went to the U.S. Supreme Court. The issue before the Court: Does the New York Labor Law unnecessarily interfere with the freedom to contract for labor in the bakery business?

The Supreme Court in a 5-4 decision overturned the decision of the state courts and issued an opinion in favor of Lochner. This narrow margin reflected several changes of opinion since the Court's 1898 decision in *Holden v. Hardy*. Apparently, a last-minute witness changed the minds of Justice Henry Billings Brown and Chief Justice Melville Fuller. In the *Holden* case, both had voted with the majority to uphold the right of the state of Utah to protect its citizens by regulating hours of work in the mining industry. The *Lochner* decision went the other way, firmly supporting **laissez-faire** attitudes toward business.

In this case, the majority decided that baking was not dangerous enough to merit interference by the state legislature. They concluded that, except in dangerous jobs, limits on working hours were "meddlesome interferences with the rights of the individual." Referring to the idea of liberty of contract, Justice Rufus Peckham wrote for the majority:

> The statute necessarily interferes with the right of contract between the employer and employees, concerning the number of hours in which the latter may labor in the bakery of the employer. The general right to make a contract in relation to his business is part of the liberty of the individual protected by the 14th Amendment. . . .

The Court did not see the law as an issue of public health, since it protected only bakers. This made it a labor law, which they could not uphold. Peckham's opinion continued:

> Clean and wholesome bread does not depend upon whether the baker works but ten hours a day or only sixty hours a week. . . . There is, in our judgment, no reasonable foundation for holding this to be necessary or appropriate as a health law to safeguard the public health, or the health of the individuals who are following the trade of a baker. . . . We think that there can be no fair doubt that the trade of a bak-

Supreme Court Decision 10

er, in and of itself, is not an unhealthy one to that degree which would authorize the legislature to interfere with the right to labor, and with the right of contract on the part of the individual, either as employer or employee. . . . It might be safely affirmed that almost all occupations more or less affect the health. There must be more than the mere fact of the possible existence of some small amount of unhealthiness to warrant legislative interference with liberty.

The opinions of two of the dissenting justices brought up important points. As a group, they thought that the courts should generally accept a state legislature's judgment on the need for legislation. In this case, the legislators had found that health hazards did justify a law. On this point, Justice John Marshall Harlan wrote in dissent:

A decision that the New York statute is void under the 14th Amendment will, in my opinion, involve consequences of a far-reaching and mischievous character; for such a decision would seriously cripple the inherent power of the states to care for the lives, health, and well-being of their citizens.

Justice Oliver Wendell Holmes also dissented. His opinion questioned the liberty of contract standard and showed changing attitudes toward social and economic legislation:

This case is decided upon an economic theory which a large part of the country does not entertain [support]. . . . It is settled by various decisions of this court that state constitutions and state laws may regulate life in many ways which we as legislators might think as injudicious . . . as this, and which equally with this, interfere with the liberty to contract. . . . The liberty of the citizen to do as he likes so long as he does not interfere with the liberty of others to do the same . . . is interfered with by school laws, by the Post office, by every state or municipal institution which takes his money for purposes thought desirable, whether he likes it or not. . . . But a constitution is not intended to embody a particular economic theory, whether of paternalism and the organic relation of the citizen to the state or of laissez faire. It is made for people of fundamentally differing views. . . .

Like the dissenting justices, many others saw the *Lochner* decision as an economic decision that favored employers over employees. In an era when the Progressives were working hard to eliminate social and economic evils—such as long hours and unhealthful conditions—created by the Industrial Revolution, this decision was a setback. On the other hand, Justice Harlan's argument that dangerous working conditions justified legislation would soon become a stronger force in court decisions about these kinds of laws.

Name _____ Date _____

Lochner v. New York (1905)

Elements of the Case

Directions: Fill in the appropriate information for each of the following elements of this case.

1. State the issue before the Supreme Court in this case.

_____

_____

_____

_____

_____

2. What facts of the case were presented to the Court?

_____

_____

_____

_____

_____

3. What was the decision of the Court? What was the rationale behind it?

_____

_____

_____

_____

4. What was the effect of the decision?

_____

_____

_____

_____

Supreme Court Decision 10

Name _____

Evaluation of the Case

Directions: Use your own judgment to evaluate the justices' decision and state your opinion of that decision.

1. In your opinion, did the Court make the proper decision in the *Lochner* case? Explain.

_____

_____

_____

_____

_____

2. Do you think that the state legislature or the Supreme Court would be better qualified to judge working hours and conditions in a local industry? Explain.

_____

_____

_____

_____

_____

3. Explain in your own words the doctrine of liberty of contract? Do you think this doctrine is realistic? Fair?

_____

_____

_____

_____

Supreme Court Decision 11

Dred Scott v. Sanford (1857)
Teacher Lesson Plan

Rationale

This lesson is designed to explore with students some of the issues and events in the period leading up to the Civil War, particularly the debate over slavery in the mid-19th century. This landmark Supreme Court decision raised questions about the citizenship of black Americans as well as the issue of slavery in U.S. states and territories.

General Goals

This case study will provide students with opportunities to:

1. explore the challenges of American constitutional law
2. understand the processes and procedures of the judicial system
3. examine the role of the Supreme Court in the formation of public policy
4. explore the conflict between judicial activism and judicial restraint
5. examine the opinions of Supreme Court justices
6. demonstrate critical thinking skills

Directions

Student material is provided in four blackline masters on the following pages. These should be copied and distributed to students. They include a brief description of the *Dred Scott* case as well as questions for students to answer.

Elements of the Case presents questions to check student comprehension, providing an opportunity to review with students the central issues, the Court's decision and rationale, and the effects of the case.

Evaluation of the Case provides one or more critical thinking activities for students. In this section, students are asked to evaluate the case and express their own positions on its issues.

Answer Key and Extending the Lesson

An answer key for the questions is provided on the next page, along with suggested activities for extending the lesson.

Dred Scott v. Sanford (1857)

Answer Key

Elements of the Case

1. *Issues:* The case came to the Court with two main issues: (1) Was Dred Scott, an African American born into slavery, a citizen of the United States and entitled to sue in federal court for the protection of his rights? (2) Did Scott's residence in free territory make him a free man? The issue added during the hearings was: Is the Missouri Compromise constitutional?

2. Dred Scott, an African American, was taken as a slave into Illinois, a free state, and into upper Louisiana Territory, part of the territory declared free by the Missouri Compromise. Scott later sued for his freedom, claiming that his residence in these free lands had made him a free man. Missouri courts at first agreed with him, but the state supreme court ruled that African Americans could not be citizens and so could not bring lawsuits. The case went to the Supreme Court when Scott technically had a new "owner" who lived in a different state.

3. By a 7–2 vote, the Court ruled that Scott was the property of Sanford, who was entitled to keep his property wherever he went; it also ruled that Scott was not and could not be a citizen and so was prohibited from suing in court. Chief Justice Taney then went beyond these issues and said in his opinion that the Missouri Compromise itself was unconstitutional.

4. The Dred Scott decision was controversial, welcomed in the South and denounced in the North. It increased sectional tensions leading up to the outbreak of the Civil War. The decision was the first in 54 years to declare an act of Congress unconstitutional.

Evaluation of the Case

1. Answers will vary, depending in part on students' knowledge of the history of this period. They may deduce that Taney was a southerner or at least sympathized with southern slaveowners.

2. Answers will vary but should show that students have found and read the relevant sections carefully. They should note that the Constitution does not actually define who is a citizen; slaves and Native Americans are not considered citizens, but free African Americans are not mentioned.

3. Answers should show an understanding of the meaning of national citizenship; students should also note that the Constitution allows states to determine voter qualifications but does not mention citizenship.

Extending the Lesson

1. Many legal authorities think that Chief Justice Taney went beyond the opinions of the Court majority in deciding that the Missouri Compromise was unconstitutional. Assign a small group of students to research the life and career of this important jurist and report to the class. Did Taney's background and personal opinions play a role in his decision? In what other major Supreme Court cases did he play an important part?

2. If your state is one admitted to the Union in this period of history, was it a free state or slave state? Have students research the political questions regarding slavery raised at the time your state achieved statehood.

3. There are some questions still remaining about the facts in the *Dred Scott* case. For example, it has been suggested that John Sanford was an abolitionist who did not actually purchase Scott and his family but used the situation to allow the case to be tested in the federal courts. Students may also be curious to discover what happened to Dred Scott. Have students research to see what they can find out.

Dred Scott v. Sanford (1857)

Vocabulary

Missouri Compromise An act of Congress passed in 1820 to keep a balance between the number of slave and free states; it allowed Missouri to enter the Union as a slave state and Maine to enter as a free state; the agreement excluded slavery from the Louisiana Territory north of 36° 30' (the southern boundary of Missouri).

popular sovereignty Principle that the power to govern belongs to the people, who can then grant it to the government of their choice.

Reviewing the Case

Dred Scott was an African-American man born into slavery in Missouri. Scott was considered the property of Dr. Emerson, an army surgeon, and traveled with him to several army posts. In 1834, Scott went with Emerson to Rock Island, Illinois, a free state in which slavery was not allowed. In 1836, Emerson and his household moved to Fort Snelling in the upper Louisiana Territory (near present-day St. Paul, Minnesota). Under the **Missouri Compromise**, slavery was prohibited in that territory. In 1838, Emerson returned to the state of Missouri, taking with him Scott, Scott's wife Harriet, and their daughter Eliza. Emerson had purchased Harriet from another officer. After the return to Missouri, a second daughter, Lizzie, was born. Dr. Emerson died there.

In 1846, with the help of lawyers in the antislavery movement, Scott sued Emerson's widow in a Missouri court. He asked the court to declare him free because he had been a resident of a free state and a free territory. The lower court declared Scott a free man, but the Missouri Supreme Court reversed the decision in 1852.

Instead of appealing this decision directly to the Supreme Court, Scott's legal advisers then sued John Sanford of New York, Mrs. Emerson's brother, who had become Scott's legal owner. (Court records misspelled his name as *Sandford*, and it appears that way in many reports.) Because the case now involved citizens of two states, it could be heard in the federal circuit court for Missouri.

Sanford's lawyers challenged Scott's right to sue, saying that an African American could not be a citizen. The federal court ruled that Scott's status in Missouri depended on state law, not on where he had lived or had traveled. A jury found in favor of Sanford. Scott's attorneys then appealed to the U.S. Supreme Court, charging that the circuit court had erred in its decision.

The case now involved several issues: (1) Was Dred Scott a citizen of the United States and thereby entitled to sue in federal court for the protection of his rights? (2) Did Scott's residence in free territory make him a free man? This second issue had become very controversial throughout the country. In some northern states, where antislavery feelings were strong, a slave was considered free as soon as he or she stepped onto free territory.

When the case was argued before the Supreme Court, another issue was added: Was it constitutional for Congress, through the Missouri Compromise, to ban slavery in the territories?

After months of debate, the Court, by a 7–2 vote, ruled against Scott, issuing one of the most controversial decisions of its history. Chief Justice Roger B. Taney wrote the decision, but all the justices commented. The majority opinion declared that as a person of African descent, Scott was not—and could not be—a citizen and so was not entitled to sue in federal court. The Court's decision considered Scott (and all slaves) to be property. To consider Scott a free man by his presence in a free territory or for Congress to pass an act declaring him free would be to allow the property of a citizen to be taken without due process of law. Slavery, according to the majority opinion, was a matter for state law.

Finally, Taney's opinion ruled that the Missouri Compromise was unconstitutional. Congress, he said, did not have the authority to prohibit slavery in the territories. What was more, Congress could not authorize the territorial legislatures to outlaw slavery. Here is part of Taney's opinion:

> And no words can be found in the Constitution which give Congress a greater power over slave property, or which entitles property of that kind to less protection than property of any other description. . . .
>
> Upon these considerations, it is the opinion of the court that the act of Congress which prohibited a citizen from holding and owning property of this kind [slaves] in the territory of the United States north of the line therein mentioned, is not warranted by the Constitution, and is therefore void; and that neither Dred Scott himself, nor any of his family, were made free by being carried into this territory. . . .

The other majority justices agreed that Dred Scott remained a slave though they did not support all of Taney's points. The two dissenting justices, John McLean and Benjamin Curtis, disagreed on most points, particularly on the issues of black citizenship and the legality of the Missouri Compromise.

The *Dred Scott* decision was significant and controversial for many reasons. First, the Supreme Court declared an act of Congress unconstitutional, which it had not done since *Marbury v. Madison* in 1803. Second, it heightened the tension between northern and southern states over the question of slavery. To the delight of the South and to the angry denunciation of the North, the Court declared Congress had no right to determine the limits on slavery's expansion into the territories. In declaring the Missouri Compromise unconstitutional, it limited **popular sovereignty**, saying that people in the territories could not vote on whether they wanted their state to be slave or free.

Third, the increased tensions may have hastened the coming of the Civil War. Fourth, African Americans did not recieve the rights granted in the Constitution until after the Civil War when Amendment Thirteen, which abolished slavery, and Amendment Fourteen, which granted citizenship to African Americans, were passed.

Dred Scott v. Sanford (1857)

Elements of the Case

Directions: Fill in the appropriate information for each of the following elements of this case.

1. State the issue before the Supreme Court in this case.

_____

_____

_____

_____

_____

2. What facts of the case were presented to the Court?

_____

_____

_____

_____

_____

3. What was the decision of the Court? What was the rationale behind it?

_____

_____

_____

_____

_____

4. What was the effect of the decision?

_____

_____

_____

_____

Evaluation of the Case

Directions: Use your own judgment to evaluate the justices' decision and state your opinion of that decision.

1. In your opinion, could the outcome of the case have been politically motivated? Explain.

_____

_____

_____

_____

_____

2. Read the parts of the Constitution that pertain to the slavery question. What do you think the framers of the Constitution actually did intend about the citizenship status of African Americans? Explain.

_____

_____

_____

_____

_____

3. In the decision of the Court, Justice Taney stated that if the slave states did not recognize slaves as citizens of the state, they could not be citizens of the United States. Does this mean that each individual state has the right to determine citizenship? What effect would this have on the country? Explain.

_____

_____

_____

_____

_____

Supreme Court Decision 12

Plessy v. Ferguson (1896)
Teacher Lesson Plan

Rationale

This lesson is designed to explore with students the social and political changes that occurred after the Civil War, particularly the changing legal and social status of African Americans. This Supreme Court decision supported legalized segregation and established the "separate but equal" doctrine that would be followed for many decades.

General Goals

This case study will provide students with opportunities to:

1. explore the challenges of American constitutional law
2. understand the processes and procedures of the judicial system
3. examine the role of the Supreme Court in the formation of public policy
4. explore the conflict between judicial activism and judicial restraint
5. examine the opinions of Supreme Court justices
6. demonstrate critical thinking skills

Directions

Student material is provided in four blackline masters on the following pages. These should be copied and distributed to students. They include a brief description of the *Plessy* case as well as questions for students to answer.

Elements of the Case presents questions to check student comprehension, providing an opportunity to review with students the central issues, the Court's decision and rationale, and the effects of the case.

Evaluation of the Case provides one or more critical thinking activities for students. In this section, students are asked to evaluate the case and express their own positions on its issues.

Answer Key and Extending the Lesson

An answer key for the questions is provided on the next page, along with suggested activities for extending the lesson.

Plessy v. Ferguson (1896)

Answer Key

Elements of the Case

1. *Issue:* Does the Louisiana statute establishing separate railroad cars or sections for black and white passengers violate the Thirteenth and Fourteenth Amendments and exceed the lawful police powers of the state?

2. An 1890 Louisiana law established separate railroad cars or sections for black and white passengers; sitting in the wrong part of the train was punishable by a fine or short jail term. Homer Plessy, who was one-eighth African American, bought a first class ticket and boarded the train car reserved for whites in New Orleans, Louisiana. He was asked to move, refused, and was arrested and jailed for violation of the law. He appealed on the ground that the law was unconstitutional as it was in violation of the Thirteenth and Fourteenth Amendments.

3. The Court affirmed the lower court decisions: the law did not violate the Thirteenth Amendment, as it did not impose any involuntary servitude; it did not violate the Fourteenth Amendment because if offered "separate but equal" accommodations; and it was within the powers of a state to make laws that followed established social traditions.

4. The decision in *Plessy* established the "separate but equal" doctrine as the law of land. The doctrine persisted until the growing civil rights movement of the 1950s and 1960s overturned it and the laws that had grown out of it.

Evaluation of the Case

1. Answers will vary, but most students today will find the idea of segregated trains, etc., simply not part of today's society. Some, however, may have acquired other ideas about segregation from older family members.

2. Students answers should show that they realize that the "Jim Crow" laws of this period contradicted American ideals of democracy and equality, despite this Supreme Court ruling. They should note that while Americans today do possess greater civil liberties than people in most other countries, there are still abuses in the system.

3. Answers will vary depending on students' own background and experience.

Extending the Lesson

1. Have students research, through photographs and other sources, what the supposedly equal accommodations supplied to black Americans in schools, railroad stations, etc., were actually like. Many photographic documentaries exist showing these conditions, which persisted well past their official end in the 1950s and 1960s.

2. Have students research the origin and effect of various "Jim Crow" laws on southern African Americans after reconstruction. How did these laws reverse some of the gains made after the Civil War?

Plessy v. Ferguson (1896)

Vocabulary

affirm   To agree or support, as when a higher court agrees with the earlier decision of a lower court.

"Jim Crow" laws   State laws introduced in the South after reconstruction to give official support to segregation.

Reviewing the Case

On June 7, 1892, Homer Plessy purchased a first-class ticket for a train of the East Louisiana Railway, traveling from New Orleans to Covington, Louisiana. Plessy was of mixed Caucasian and African descent, having had one black great-grandparent. Although Plessy looked white, he was considered black under state law. Plessy took a seat in a car reserved exclusively for white passengers but was told by the conductor that he would have to move to the car for African Americans. Plessy refused to move. The conductor then called local police, who removed Plessy from the train and put him in jail.

Plessy's arrest and imprisonment were based on an 1890 act of the Louisiana legislature. The law required separate railroad cars for "the white and colored races." It said that all railway companies carrying passengers in Louisiana must provide "equal but separate accommodations" for the different races, either by having at least two cars on the train or by dividing a single car with a partition.

No one was to be allowed to occupy a coach other than the one assigned to him or her by train officials. Any passenger who insisted on going into the wrong coach or compartment could be fined $25 or put in jail for up to twenty days.

Plessy pleaded not guilty to the charges against him but was convicted. He appealed to the state supreme court on the grounds that the law was unconstitutional because it conflicted with both the Thirteenth and Fourteenth Amendments. The state supreme court, however, **affirmed** the decision of the trial court. Plessy then asked the U. S. Supreme Court to review the case. The issue before the Court: Does the Louisiana statute establishing separate railroad cars or sections for black and white passengers violate the Thirteenth and Fourteenth Amendments and exceed the lawful police powers of the state?

The Supreme Court ruled by a 7–1 vote to affirm the decisions of the lower courts against Plessy. Justice Henry Brown wrote the majority opinion. The only dissenting vote was Justice John Marshall Harlan, who often voted to uphold black civil rights in cases of this era. (Harlan was the grandfather of Justice John Marshall Harlan who served on the Court from 1955 to 1971.) One justice did not hear the case or participate in the decision.

In the majority opinion, the Court ruled that the Thirteenth Amendment (which was not the main point of Plessy's case) did not apply because the restriction on seating in no way established any condition of "involuntary servitude." More importantly, the Court ruled that the Louisiana law did not violate the Fourteenth Amendment because it did not restrict blacks any differently from whites. Each race merely had to use its assigned, separate accommodations on the railways. The justices also believed that states had the right and power to follow established social customs and traditions in restricting the mixing of the races in transportation, schools, and other situations.

Justice Brown, referring to the Fourteenth Amendment, wrote for the majority:

The object of the Amendment was undoubtedly to enforce the absolute equality of the two races before the law, but in the nature of things it could not have been intended to abolish distinctions based upon color, or to enforce social, as distinguished from political, equality, or a commingling [mixing] of the two races upon terms unsatisfactory to either. Laws permitting and even requiring their separation in places where they are liable to be brought into contact do not necessarily imply the inferiority of either race to the other, and have been generally, if not universally, recognized as within the competency of the state legislatures in the exercise of their police power.

Justice John Marshall Harlan, however, saw the intent of the Fourteenth Amendment differently. He wrote in his eloquent dissenting opinion:

. . . in view of the Constitution, in the eye of the law, there is in this country no superior, dominant, ruling class of citizens. There is no caste here. Our Constitution is color-blind, and neither knows nor tolerates classes among citizens. In respect of civil rights, all citizens are equal before the law.
. . . The law regards man as man, and takes no account of his surroundings or of his color when his civil rights as guaranteed by the supreme law of the land are involved.

The effects of the *Plessy* decision were far-reaching. It firmly established the doctrine of "separate but equal" as the law of the land. It legitimized the segregation begun under the southern **"Jim Crow" laws** and extended the legality of those laws nationwide. "Separate but equal" remained an accepted principle for some 50 years, until the civil rights movement gained strength in the 1950's and 1960's. When it was finally overturned in 1954 (*Brown v. Board of Education*), the Court referred to this decision and to Justice Harlan's powerful dissent in which he said:

The arbitrary separation of citizens, on the basis of race, while they are on a public highway [the railroad], is a badge of servitude wholly inconsistent with the civil freedom and the equality before the law established by the Constitution. It cannot be justified upon any legal grounds.
If evils result from the commingling of the two races upon public highways established for the benefit of all, they will be infinitely less than those that will surely come from state legislation regulating the enjoyment of civil rights upon the basis of race. We boast of the freedom enjoyed by our people above all other peoples. But it is difficult to reconcile that boast with a state of the law which, practically, puts the brand of servitude and degradation upon a large class of our fellow citizens, our equals before the law. The thin disguise of "equal" accommodations for passengers in railroad coaches will not mislead anyone, or atone for the wrong this day done.

Supreme Court Decision 12

Name _____ Date _____

Plessy v. Ferguson (1896)

Elements of the Case

Directions: Fill in the appropriate information for each of the following elements of this case.

1. State the issue before the Supreme Court in this case.

_____

_____

_____

_____

2. What facts of the case were presented to the Court?

_____

_____

_____

_____

3. What was the decision of the Court? What was the rationale behind it?

_____

_____

_____

_____

4. What was the effect of the decision?

_____

_____

_____

_____

Evaluation of the Case

Directions: Use your own judgment to evaluate the justices' decision and state your opinion of that decision.

1. Compare the statements of Justices Brown and Harlan. With which did you agree? Explain.

_____

_____

_____

_____

_____

2. What do you think Justice Harlan meant when he said that Americans would find it difficult to boast about being the freest people on earth? Do you think this is still true today?

_____

_____

_____

_____

_____

3. Do you think that the long acceptance of "separate but equal" promoted the development of a "class system" in this country? Was "separate" ever really "equal"? Explain.

_____

_____

_____

_____

_____

Supreme Court Decision 13

Brown v. Board of Education of Topeka (1954)
Teacher Lesson Plan

Rationale

This lesson is designed to explore with students some of the major social and political changes that were a part of the movement to secure civil rights for all Americans. This landmark Supreme Court decision began the process of ending racial segregation in public schools, overturning the long-standing doctrine of "separate but equal" facilities for different races.

General Goals

This case study will provide students with opportunities to:

1. explore the challenges of American constitutional law
2. understand the processes and procedures of the judicial system
3. examine the role of the Supreme Court in the formation of public policy
4. explore the conflict between judicial activism and judicial restraint
5. examine the opinions of Supreme Court justices
6. demonstrate critical thinking skills

Directions

Student material is provided in four blackline masters on the following pages. These should be copied and distributed to students. They include a brief description of *Brown v. Board of Education* as well as questions for students to answer.

Elements of the Case presents questions to check student comprehension, providing an opportunity to review with students the central issues, the Court's decision and rationale, and the effects of the case.

Evaluation of the Case provides one or more critical thinking activities for students. In this section, students are asked to evaluate the case and express their own positions on its issues.

Answer Key and Extending the Lesson

An answer key for the questions is provided on the next page, along with suggested activities for extending the lesson.

Brown v. Board of Education of Topeka (1954)

Answer Key

Elements of the Case

1. *Issue*: Does racial segregation in public schools deprive minority children of equal protection of the laws under the Fourteenth Amendment?

2. The school system in Topeka, Kansas, was racially segregated; the facilities for black and white students were fairly equal in terms of buildings, books, qualified teachers, and other physical factors. It met the guidelines of *Plessy v. Ferguson* (1896), the Supreme Court case that allowed the "separate but equal" doctrine. Linda Brown's parents challenged the constitutionality of school segregation on the basis of the Fourteenth Amendment. With NAACP help, their case and other similar cases went to the Supreme Court.

3. The Court ruled that segregated schools were "inherently unequal," creating a class society in which the minority children were given a permanent sense of inferiority. The Court, therefore, overturned its decision in *Plessy*. It later put district courts in charge of seeing that desegregation took place with "all deliberate speed."

4. The decision was seen as a great victory by civil rights advocates, although implementing it took many years and many more legal actions. Many states and cities affected by the decision thought it was undue interference with a state's right to control education. The decision opened the door for much more civil rights action by African Americans and other groups.

Evaluation of the Case

1. Answers may vary, for some students may think that separate schools can provide a special cultural focus to develop racial pride and identity.

2. Answers will vary, but most students will realize that this decision opened the way for broad civil rights legislation.

3. Answers will vary but should show that students have given careful thought to the problem. Students' plans can provide the basis for class discussion.

Extending the Lesson

1. In class, have each student make a personal list of the facilities and other qualities that he or she thinks are important in a good school. Compare lists in class and compile a general class list on the chalkboard, separating material things (lab equipment, libraries, etc.) from intangibles. Encourage students to discuss which of those things could and could not be achieved in "separate but equal" schools for racial or ethnic minorities.

2. Have some students review the Supreme Court decision in *Plessy v. Ferguson* (Decision 12 in this book) and explain to the class the origins of the doctrine of "separate but equal." The schools in Topeka were considered more or less equal in physical facilities and equipment; do students believe this was generally true in the 1940s and 1950s?

3. Have students research the integration process in your state and two other states to compare the speed with which integration took place and the difficulties created for the states in complying with the decision. (For example, the crisis at Central High School in Little Rock, Arkansas, 1957)

Brown v. Board of Education of Topeka (1954)

Vocabulary

NAACP (National Association for the Advancement of Colored People)
One of the earliest civil rights organizations (founded 1909) working for political and legal rights for African Americans.

Reviewing the Case

Linda Brown was an 8-year-old girl living in the city of Topeka, Kansas, in the early 1950's. While her white neighbors went to a nearby grade school, Linda, an African American, had to take a long bus ride to a school that was segregated on the basis of race. The Topeka Board of Education had created a school system with separate schools for black and white students. Such segregated public school systems were common throughout the country at that time, some mandated by local law, some created by housing patterns or other factors.

Such systems were legal and acceptable under the doctrine of "separate but equal." For a long time, the **NAACP** and other civil rights supporters had been trying to overturn this doctrine, which had been established by the Supreme Court's 1896 decision in *Plessy v. Ferguson*. That case gave the Court's approval to segregation in transportation, housing, and other areas of society, as long as equal facilities were provided. When Linda Brown's parents sued in a federal district court, the court found that Topeka had provided fairly equal conditions in the white and black schools. With the encouragement of the NAACP, the Browns then appealed to the Supreme Court.

For some years after *Plessy*, the Supreme Court had accepted obvious inequalities between facilities for blacks and whites. From the late 1930's on, however, the justices had become stricter. The Court had found, for example, that separate law schools for African Americans were not equal either in physical facilities or in other important qualities. The Court had not yet taken a second look at the "separate but equal" doctrine itself, but these cases seemed to be leading up to it.

By the fall of 1952, the Browns' case and four other school segregation cases were awaiting the Supreme Court's review. The cases came from four states and the District of Columbia. All challenged the constitutionality of racial segregation in public schools. In most instances, the schools were fairly equal in terms of buildings, books, qualified teachers, and similar factors. The central issue was no longer the equality of those physical and tangible aspects. It was the effect that segregation itself had on the education of black children.

Did "separate but equal" schooling create a class system that offered whites a better quality of education than blacks? Did it deprive the minority children of equal educational opportunities? The issue as presented before the Court: Does racial segregation of children in public schools deprive minority children of equal protection of the laws under the Fourteenth Amendment?

The Court ruled unanimously to overturn its decision in *Plessy v. Ferguson*. In writing the majority opinion, Chief Justice Earl Warren discussed the importance of education in children's development:

> Today, education is perhaps the most important function of state and local governments. . . . It is the very foundation of good citizenship. Today it is a principal instrument in awakening the child to cultural values, in preparing him for later professional training, and in helping him to adjust normally to his environment. In these days it is doubtful that any child may reasonably be expected to succeed in life if he is denied the opportunity of an education. Such an opportunity, where the state has undertaken to provide it, is a right which must be made available to all on equal terms.

We come then to the question presented: Does segregation of children in public schools solely on the basis of race, even though the physical facilities and other "tangible" factors may be equal, deprive the children of the minority group of equal educational opportunities? We believe that it does.

Warren referred to some of the segregation cases that had involved college students, then pointed out that the situation was more severe for younger children:

To separate them from others of similar age and qualifications solely because of their race generates a feeling of inferiority as to their status in the community that may affect their hearts and minds in a way unlikely ever to be undone.

In conclusion, the opinion said:

Any language in *Plessy v. Ferguson* contrary to this finding is rejected. We conclude that in the field of public education the doctrine of 'separate but equal' has no place. Separate educational facilities are inherently unequal.

The Court recognized that eliminating the segregated school systems was a complex problem that would vary from place to place. Now that the Court had settled the primary question—the unconstitutional nature of segregated education—it set a date for later hearings and discussions.

A year later, the Court issued a second ruling on *Brown v. Board of Education of Topeka*, often called "Brown II." It sent all the specific cases back to the district courts, which it was felt could give better consideration to local issues. The decision emphasized "good faith compliance" and urged the ending of public school segregation "with all deliberate speed."

This case was a great victory for supporters of civil rights. Local school boards and state officials, however, saw it as a serious infringement of a state's right to oversee education. The decision provided a solid legal basis for erasing segregation in other areas of daily life, such as employment and housing. Still, resistance to change was strong, and school systems in many places remained segregated for many years after the *Brown* decision.

Name _____ Date _____

Brown v. Board of Education of Topeka (1954)

Elements of the Case

Directions: Fill in the appropriate information for each of the following elements of this case.

1. State the issue before the Supreme Court in this case.

_____

_____

_____

_____

2. What facts of the case were presented to the Court?

_____

_____

_____

_____

3. What was the decision of the Court? What was the rationale behind it?

_____

_____

_____

_____

4. What was the effect of the decision?

_____

_____

_____

_____

Supreme Court Decision 13

Name _____   *Brown v. Board of Education of Topeka* (cont.)

Evaluation of the Case

Directions: Use your own judgment to evaluate the justices' decision and state your opinion of that decision.

1. Do you agree with the opinion of the Court in this case? Do you think that it is possible to have segregated schools that can actually offer equal educational chances? Explain.

_____

_____

_____

_____

_____

2. What effect do you think the *Brown* decision had on related issues such as women's rights, equal opportunities for other minorities (such as Hispanics or Native Americans), or opportunities and access for the handicapped? Explain.

_____

_____

_____

_____

_____

3. Imagine that you were given the task of planning the desegregation of a city school system that had always had dual schools for blacks and whites. How would you go about it? Outline the plan you would follow.

_____

_____

_____

_____

_____

Supreme Court Decision 13

Supreme Court Decision 14

Betts v. Brady (1942)
Teacher Lesson Plan

Rationale

This lesson is designed to explore with students the background of some of the changes in criminal procedure brought about by the Warren Court. This 1942 case concerned the right of those accused of crimes to have an attorney represent them at the time of trial. This Supreme Court decision, however, placed strict limits on that right that would not be overturned until *Gideon v. Wainwright* in 1963.

General Goals

This case study will provide students with opportunities to:

1. explore the challenges of American constitutional law
2. understand the processes and procedures of the judicial system
3. examine the role of the Supreme Court in the formation of public policy
4. explore the conflict between judicial activism and judicial restraint
5. examine the opinions of Supreme Court justices
6. demonstrate critical thinking skills

Directions

Student material is provided in four blackline masters on the following pages. These should be copied and distributed to students. They include a brief description of *Betts v. Brady* as well as questions for students to answer.

Elements of the Case presents questions to check student comprehension, providing an opportunity to review with students the central issues, the Court's decision and rationale, and the effects of the case.

Evaluation of the Case provides one or more critical thinking activities for students. In this section, students are asked to evaluate the case and express their own positions on its issues.

Answer Key and Extending the Lesson

An answer key for the questions is provided on the next page, along with suggested activities for extending the lesson.

Betts v. Brady (1942)

Answer Key

Elements of the Case

1. *Issue:* Did the courts of Maryland violate the defendant's right to counsel under the Sixth Amendment to the Constitution and thereby also violate his Fourteenth Amendment guarantee of due process?

2. Smith Betts could not afford an attorney and was denied a court-appointed attorney to defend him against a robbery charge brought against him in Carroll County, Maryland. He argued that the conviction should be overturned and he should be released from prison on the grounds that the judge violated his Sixth Amendment right to counsel and his Fourteenth Amendment right to due process. The judge refused because Betts was of average intelligence and had been in court before.

3. The Court ruled 6-3 to affirm the decision of the lower court, making no "hard and fast rule" that would govern how and when the Fourteenth Amendment applied to cases in state courts. They chose to follow the interpretation established in *Powell v. Alabama* (1932). Under those rules, court-appointed attorneys would have to be provided only for defendants charged with a capital crime or in "special circumstances" such as being illiterate or mentally handicapped.

4. For some years after this decision, many indigent defendants were tried in state courts without legal counsel and as a result were convicted and sent to prison.

Evaluation of the Case

1. Answers will vary, but students should be clear on the distinction between the protections that apply to the federal government (Bill of Rights) and those that have been made applicable to the states.

2. Answers will vary, depending in part on students' own backgrounds and experience with the criminal justice system. If students require the provision of attorneys only in certain cases, have them discuss their choices and exceptions.

3. Answers will vary, as many students may think they could defend themselves.

Extending the Lesson

1. In connection with both this case and with *Gideon v. Wainwright* (Decision 15), have students read and report on the book *Gideon's Trumpet* (1964), by Anthony Lewis. The book is an engrossing account of the case that overturned this decision. It contains considerable background and many references to the *Betts* case.

2. If possible, arrange for students to attend a courtroom trial for a criminal case and observe exactly what the defense attorneys do as the case proceeds. If attending court is not practical, arrange for students to watch televised court proceedings, preferably real cases rather than TV dramas or reenactments. Have them keep in mind the importance of counsel from the defendant's point of view.

Betts v. Brady (1942)

Vocabulary

counsel   Legal advice or representation.

(writ of) habeas corpus   Court order requiring that a person in custody be brought before a court so a judge can determine the legality of keeping him or her in jail.

precedent   An earlier court decision used as a guide or model in deciding similar cases.

capital crime   Crime for which the death sentence can be imposed.

Reviewing the Case

Smith Betts was a 43-year-old farm worker, unemployed and on welfare, when he was charged with robbery in Carroll County, Maryland. Because he was without money to secure **counsel**, Betts asked the judge to appoint an attorney to represent him. The judge refused because the local practice was to appoint lawyers only for charges of murder or rape. Betts defended himself in court and was convicted of robbery.

Betts then appealed to the highest state court for a writ of **habeas corpus**. He alleged that he had been denied his Sixth Amendment right to counsel and that the court's denial of representation had violated the Fourteenth Amendment's guarantee of due process. He asked the court to order his conviction overturned and his release from prison. Chief Judge Carroll Bond refused, saying that the right to counsel was not a fundamental right and that the Sixth Amendment did not apply to the states.

Judge Bond also pointed out that Betts was not helpless. He was an adult, of average intelligence, and not completely unfamiliar with court procedure because he had been tried for larceny on an earlier occasion and had been convicted. The judge felt that Betts was capable of putting on an adequate and appropriate defense for himself.

Unsuccessful in the state courts, Betts turned to the United States Supreme Court. The issue before the Court: Did the courts of Maryland violate the defendant's right to counsel under the Sixth Amendment and thereby also violate the Fourteenth Amendment guarantee of due process?

The Court decided by a vote of 6–3 to affirm the decision of the Maryland state courts. Agreeing generally with Judge Bond, the Court ruled that the due process clause of the Fourteenth Amendment does not necessarily extend the Sixth Amendment to state courts. Therefore, the states are not always required to provide lawyers for defendants who are too poor to pay for counsel.

Justice Owen Roberts, writing for the majority of the Court, chose to make no "hard and fast rule" concerning the states in this area. The justices decided in accordance with the **precedent** set ten years earlier in *Powell v. Alabama* (1932). In that case, the Supreme Court had ruled that there were "common and fundamental ideas of fairness and right" that should guide the state courts in this matter.

Court-appointed attorneys, it said, should be provided for a defendant charged with a **capital crime** or one in certain "special circumstances." These circumstances applied, for instance, to defendants who were illiterate, mentally handicapped, or totally ignorant of the law and court procedure. The Court did not think that Betts met any of these requirements.

Justice Hugo Black, along with Justices Douglas and Murphy, was one of the dissenting justices. Believing that the right to counsel was fundamental to a fair trial, Black wrote:

I believe the Fourteenth Amendment made the Sixth applicable to the states. . . . A practice cannot be reconciled with "common and fundamental fairness and right" which subjects innocent men to increased dangers of conviction merely because of their poverty. . . . denial of counsel has made it impossible to conclude, with any satisfactory degree of certainty, that the defendant's case was adequately presented.

Black concluded that no one should be deprived of legal counsel simply because of poverty. "Any other practice," he said, "seems to me to defeat the promise of our democratic society to provide equal justice under the law."

As a result of the Betts ruling, many poor defendants would go on trial in state courts without attorneys to represent them. The decision was widely criticized. One prominent lawyer of the time pointed out that the decision seemed badly timed since, in 1942, Americans and their allies were fighting to assure people their fundamental democratic rights. Nevertheless, *Betts v. Brady* remained the Court's rule for the next twenty years.

Betts v. Brady (1942)

Elements of the Case

Directions: Fill in the appropriate information for each of the following elements of this case.

1. State the issue before the Supreme Court in this case.

_____

_____

_____

_____

_____

2. What facts of the case were presented to the Court?

_____

_____

_____

_____

3. What was the decision of the Court? What was the rationale behind it?

_____

_____

_____

_____

4. What was the effect of the decision?

_____

_____

_____

_____

Name _____

Evaluation of the Case

Directions: Use your own judgment to evaluate the justices' decision and state your opinion of that decision.

1. Do you agree with the majority opinion in this case or do you agree with Justice Black, who wrote in dissent? Explain your position.

_____

_____

_____

_____

_____

2. Did this decision, in your opinion, place justice out of reach for the poor of this country? Should the state be required to appoint an attorney for poor people in all types of criminal cases? Why do you think as you do?

_____

_____

_____

_____

_____

3. Try to imagine yourself in Smith Betts's position. Do you think that you could effectively defend yourself in court without the help of a lawyer? Explain how you would do so.

_____

_____

_____

_____

_____

Supreme Court Decision 15

Gideon v. Wainwright (1963)
Teacher Lesson Plan

Rationale

This lesson is designed to explore with students some of the changes in criminal procedure made under the Warren Court, specifically those that strengthened the constitutional protections (in the Sixth Amendment) for the rights of persons accused of crimes. This landmark Supreme Court case established the right to counsel as a fundamental right in all criminal cases, state or federal.

General Goals

This case study will provide students with opportunities to:

1. explore the challenges of American constitutional law
2. understand the processes and procedures of the judicial system
3. examine the role of the Supreme Court in the formation of public policy
4. explore the conflict between judicial activism and judicial restraint
5. examine the opinions of Supreme Court justices
6. demonstrate critical thinking skills

Directions

Student material is provided in four blackline masters on the following pages. These should be copied and distributed to students. They include a brief description of the *Gideon* case as well as questions for students to answer.

Elements of the Case presents questions to check student comprehension, providing an opportunity to review with students the central issues, the Court's decision and rationale, and the effects of the case.

Evaluation of the Case provides one or more critical thinking activities for students. In this section, students are asked to evaluate the case and express their own positions on its issues.

Answer Key and Extending the Lesson

An answer key for the questions is provided on the next page, along with suggested activities for extending the lesson.

Gideon v. Wainwright (1963)

Answer Key

Elements of the Case

1. *Issue:* Should the Court overrule *Betts v. Brady* (1942) and declare that the due process clause of the Fourteenth Amendment obligates the states to apply the Sixth Amendment in all criminal cases?
2. Gideon was charged with breaking into and entering a pool hall with the intent to rob it. He asked the court to appoint an attorney for him because he did not have the money to pay for one and because he believed the U.S. Supreme Court had ruled he was entitled to be represented. The request was denied because Florida law allowed it only for capital crimes. Gideon conducted his own defense and was found guilty. From prison, Gideon appealed in forma pauperis to the U.S. Supreme Court on the grounds that the denial of a court-appointed attorney deprived him of due process under the Sixth and Fourteenth Amendments. The Court had ruled in *Betts v. Brady* that the right to counsel did not apply in all state cases but agreed to reconsider the issue.
3. The Court voted unanimously to overrule *Betts*, declaring that the Fourteenth Amendment obligated the states to follow the Sixth Amendment and provide counsel to indigent defendants in all criminal trials.
4. Many people who had been tried without an attorney received new trials or were re-leased. At his retrial, with a court-appointed lawyer, Gideon was freed. The case set a precedent that no defendant must face trial without legal counsel even if the state must provide it.

Evaluation of the Case

1. Answers will vary, but most students' sympathies are likely to be with Gideon and other defendants.
2. If students' answers do change, they should be able to justify them: how has the basic issue of right to counsel changed?
3. Answers will vary, but most students will think that lawyers know better ways of approaching and dealing with "the system."

Extending the Lesson

1. If students have not studied *Betts v. Brady* (Decision 14 in this book), have some of them do so, then report to the class on the similarities between the cases. The other student activities suggested for *Betts* are also appropriate here.
2. Have one or more students read and report on the book *Gideon's Trumpet* (1964), by Anthony Lewis. The book is an engrossing account of not only Gideon's particular case but also about the workings of the Supreme Court. A video also entitled *Gideon's Trumpet* may be available locally for rental.

Gideon v. Wainwright (1963)

Vocabulary

counsel   Legal advice or representation.

capital crime   Crime for which the death sentence can be imposed.

(writ of) habeas corpus   Court order requiring that a person in custody be brought before a court so a judge can determine the legality of keeping him or her in jail.

writ of certiorari   An order by a higher court to a lower court requesting the records of a case for review; the usual route by which cases reach the Supreme Court.

in forma pauperis   Latin for "in the manner of a pauper [poor person]; referring to applications to the Supreme Court by those who cannot afford the usual procedures and so are allowed to proceed under special rules.

due process clause   Clause in the Fourteenth Amendment that protects every person's right to "due process of law" from interference by state governments; used to make most Bill of Rights protections apply to the states.

Reviewing the Case

Clarence Earl Gideon, an indigent 52-year-old drifter, was arrested for breaking into a pool hall in Panama City, Florida. He stood trial in a Florida state court on a charge of breaking and entering a pool hall with the intent to burglarize it. Appearing in court, Gideon asked the judge to appoint an attorney for him at state expense because he did not have the money to pay for one himself.

In response to the request, the judge told Gideon that under Florida law, he could not appoint **counsel** except in cases involving **capital crimes.** According to court records, Gideon then said, "The United States Supreme Court says I am entitled to be represented by counsel." Without a court-appointed lawyer, Gideon then conducted his own defense as well as he could. (He had been tried and convicted on earlier occasions for minor crimes.) He made an opening statement, called witnesses on his behalf, cross-examined the prosecution's witnesses, refused to testify himself, and delivered a closing argument. He was, however, found guilty of the charge and sent to prison for five years.

In the prison library, Gideon prepared an appeal to the Florida Supreme Court. Asking for a writ of **habeas corpus,** he claimed that the judge's decision to deny him a court-appointed attorney violated rights he was guaranteed by the Constitution and the Bill of Rights. The State Supreme Court denied the appeal.

Gideon then appealed, in a handwritten letter, to the United States Supreme Court. He again based his case on the grounds that his right to counsel under the Sixth and Fourteenth Amendments had been violated. The Court issued a **writ of certiorari** to the Florida courts requesting the records of the case.

The circumstances of Gideon's trial and the similarities of his case to the Betts case made it a likely case with which to reexamine the Court's ruling in *Betts v. Brady* (1942). In that case, the Court had decided that right to counsel was not such a fundamental right that it should always be extended to state courts. However, *Betts* did require counsel for capital cases and when the defendant possessed certain "special circumstances" such as mental handicaps or illiteracy.

Because Gideon had petitioned the Supreme Court **in forma pauperis,** the Court appointed Abe Fortas to represent him and present his case to the Court. Since the Betts case had become an issue, Fortas was asked to show cause why the Court should reconsider its decision in *Betts v. Brady.*

The issue that came before the Court: Should the Court overrule *Betts v. Brady* (1942) and declare that the **due process clause** of the Fourteenth Amendment obligates the states to apply the Sixth Amendment in all criminal cases?

In addition to the state of Florida, two other states submitted statements asking the Court to uphold the Betts decision, but 22 states asked the Court to overrule it, claiming the decision was outdated even at the time it was written.

The Court ruled unanimously to overrule *Betts v. Brady* (1942). It declared that the Fourteenth Amendment obligated the states to follow the Sixth Amendment and provide counsel in to indigent defendants in all criminal trials.

Justice Hugo Black, who, 21 years before, had been one of the dissenting justices in the *Betts* decision, wrote the unanimous opinion for the Court. In this case, writing an opinion shared by all the justices, Black wrote:

We accept *Betts v. Brady*'s assumption, based as it was on our prior cases, that a provision of the Bill of Rights which is "fundamental and essential to a fair trial" is made obligatory upon the states by the Fourteenth Amendment. We think the Court in *Betts* was wrong, however, in concluding that the Sixth Amendment's guarantee of counsel is not one of these fundamental rights. . . .

The right of one charged with crime to counsel may not be deemed fundamental and essential to fair trials in some countries, but it is in ours. . . . This noble ideal cannot be realized if the poor man charged with crime has to face his accusers without a lawyer to assist him. . . .

Gideon's conviction was reversed and the case sent back to the Florida courts for further action. This decision brought the review of thousands of other cases throughout the country, in which poor defendants had been tried without legal counsel. Many people serving prison sentences were released, while others, like Clarence Earl Gideon, stood trial again. Gideon stood trial again in the same court and before the same judge and prosecutor, but with the assistance of counsel, he was found not guilty of the charges against him. He walked out of the courtroom a free man.

Because of Gideon's pauper's petition to the United States Supreme Court, no one accused of a crime has to stand trial in any court in the land without benefit of counsel unless he or she specifically refuses it. In addition, many cities have created the position of "public defender," a staff of lawyers paid by the government to defend people who cannot afford attorneys.

Name _____   Date _____

Gideon v. Wainwright (1963)

Elements of the Case

Directions: Fill in the appropriate information for each of the following elements of this case.

1. State the issue before the Supreme Court in this case.

_____

_____

_____

_____

_____

2. What facts of the case were presented to the Court?

_____

_____

_____

_____

_____

3. What was the decision of the Court? What was the rationale behind it?

_____

_____

_____

_____

_____

4. What was the effect of the decision?

_____

_____

_____

_____

Supreme Court Decision 15

Name _____

Evaluation of the Case

Directions: Use your own judgment to evaluate the justices' decision and state your opinion of that decision.

1. Do you agree that the Court made the right decision in the Gideon case, or would you have upheld the earlier *Betts* decision? Explain.

_____

_____

_____

_____

_____

_____

2. Would your opinion in question 1 be different if Gideon had been found guilty upon retrial? Explain.

_____

_____

_____

_____

_____

_____

3. In your opinion, is it necessary to have a lawyer represent you in court to receive a fair trial? Explain.

_____

_____

_____

_____

_____

_____

Supreme Court Decision 16

Escobedo v. Illinois (1964)
Teacher Lesson Plan

Rationale

This lesson is designed to explore with students some of the changes in criminal procedure made under the Warren Court, specifically those that strengthened the constitutional protections (in the Sixth Amendment) for the rights of persons accused of crimes. This Supreme Court case concerned the right to have an attorney present during police questioning.

General Goals

This case study will provide students with opportunities to:

1. explore the challenges of American constitutional law
2. understand the processes and procedures of the judicial system
3. examine the role of the Supreme Court in the formation of public policy
4. explore the conflict between judicial activism and judicial restraint
5. examine the opinions of Supreme Court justices
6. demonstrate critical thinking skills

Directions

Student material is provided in four blackline masters on the following pages. These should be copied and distributed to students. They include a brief description of the *Escobedo* case as well as questions for students to answer.

Elements of the Case presents questions to check student comprehension, providing an opportunity to review with students the central issues, the Court's decision and rationale, and the effects of the case.

Evaluation of the Case provides one or more critical thinking activities for students. In this section, students are asked to evaluate the case and express their own positions on its issues.

Answer Key and Extending the Lesson

An answer key for the questions is provided on the next page, along with suggested activities for extending the lesson.

Escobedo v. Illinois (1964)

Answer Key

Elements of the Case

1. *Issue:* Was the refusal by police to honor Escobedo's request to consult with his lawyer a violation of his Sixth Amendment rights?
2. Danny Escobedo, a suspect in the murder of his brother-in-law, was picked up twice by police for questioning. He asked for his lawyer to be present, and his lawyer asked to see him, but both were told to wait until the questioning was over. During police questioning, Escobedo made statements that incriminated him. Although a motion was made to suppress the statements as evidence, he was convicted of murder. Police said he had given the information voluntarily, and the courts upheld his conviction.
3. The U. S. Supreme Court reversed the Illinois courts. The majority decision made a distinction about the point at which an investigation becomes "accusatory," and suspects are entitled to have an attorney present unless they waive that right. The evidence was not allowed.
4. The Escobedo decision was controversial. It extended the right of the accused to have an attorney present during questioning by police. Information obtained without this right was inadmissible in court. Many law enforcement officials and four Supreme Court justices thought it made convictions more difficult for police and prosecutors.

Evaluation of the Case

1. Answers will vary depending on students' orientation and attitudes toward law enforcement.
2. Answers will vary but should show that students understand the need to balance law enforcement with the constitutional rights of citizens.
3. Answers should show that students have given thought to both sides in this question.

Extending the Lesson

1. Have students read the cases in this book concerning the 1960s decisions concerning the rights of the accused: *Gideon v. Wainwright*, *Escobedo v. Illinois*, *Miranda v. Arizona* (Decisions 15, 16, 17). The Warren Court was criticized by some for "protecting criminals." Have students debate whether they think the Court was defending individual rights or giving criminals too much leeway.
2. If possible, invite a police officer or prosecuting attorney to discuss the limits that law enforcement personnel must observe in giving suspects their Sixth Amendment rights. Do they think these laws are burdensome or unnecessary?

Escobedo v. Illinois (1964)

Vocabulary

(writ of) habeas corpus Court order requiring that a person in custody be brought before a court so a judge can determine the legality of keeping him or her in jail.

incriminate To involve in or charge with a crime or other illegal act.

suppress In court, to not allow certain evidence to be presented.

Reviewing the Case

Danny Escobedo's brother-in-law was killed on January 19, 1960. At about 2:30 in the morning, Escobedo was arrested without a warrant and taken to the Chicago police headquarters for questioning. Escobedo made no statement to the police and was released at approximately 5:00 that afternoon, after his lawyer obtained a writ of **habeas corpus.**

Ten days later, on January 30, Escobedo was again arrested, handcuffed, and driven to the police station. On the way to the station, the police allegedly informed Escobedo that a man named Benedict DiGerlando had said it was Escobedo who had fired the shots that killed his brother-in-law. The police also allegedly told Escobedo that the case against him was pretty secure and he might as well "come clean" and admit to the killing. At that point, Escobedo asked to have his lawyer present before answering any questions.

The police questioned Escobedo for several hours, during which he continued to ask for his attorney. He was told that he could do so after the police concluded their interrogation. Escobedo's attorney, who was at the police station on another matter, discovered that Escobedo was in custody. He asked repeatedly to speak to his client but got the same answer: He could see Escobedo after the questioning.

While interrogating Escobedo, the police told him that they had DiGerlando in custody. They asked Escobedo if he would like to call DiGerlando a liar to his face. Escobedo said he would, and when the two men met,

Escobedo said to DiGerlando: "I didn't shoot Manuel—you did." This statement placed Escobedo at the crime scene for the first time or, at the least, showed that he had knowledge of the crime. As the questioning continued, Escobedo gave other information that **incriminated** himself, his sister, and DiGerlando in the murder of his brother-in-law.

Before his trial, and on appeal, Escobedo asked the court to **suppress** all information gathered during the interrogation without his attorney. The motion was denied, and Escobedo was convicted of the murder of his brother-in-law.

In February 1963, the Illinois Supreme Court heard Escobedo's appeal, ruled that the information should not have been allowed as evidence, and reversed the decision of the lower court. However, the state appealed for a rehearing. Saying that Escobedo had given the information voluntarily, the state asked the court to rule in favor of the prosecution and admit the evidence. The court agreed.

Escobedo then petitioned the United States Supreme Court to review the case. The issue before the Court: Was the refusal by police to honor Escobedo's request to consult with his lawyer a violation of his Sixth Amendment rights?

The U. S. Supreme Court, by a vote of 5–4, said that Escobedo's rights had been violated. Overturning the ruling of the state supreme court, it declared that the information was not admissible as evidence because it had been unlawfully obtained.

Writing for the Court, Justice Arthur Goldberg explained the point at which a police procedure became "accusatory" instead of "investigatory:"

. . .[when] the investigation is no longer a general inquiry into an unsolved crime but has begun to focus on a particular subject, . . . the police carry out a process of interrogation that lends itself to eliciting incriminating statements, the suspect has requested and been denied an opportunity to consult with his lawyer, and the police have not effectively warned him of his absolute constitutional right to remain silent, the accused has been denied "the Assistance of Counsel" in violation of the Sixth Amendment. . . .[N]o statement elicited by the police during the interrogation may be used against him at a criminal trial.

The dissenting justices expressed their serious concerns that this decision would make it much more difficult for the police to obtain information and for prosecutors to gain convictions.

Writing in dissent, Justice John Marshall Harlan stated:

I would affirm the judgment of the Supreme Court of Illinois. . . . I think the rule announced today is most ill-conceived and that it seriously and unjustly fetters perfectly legitimate methods of criminal law enforcement.

Justice Byron White wrote the dissenting opinion for himself and Justices Clark and Stewart:

I do not suggest for a moment that law enforcement will be destroyed by the rule announced today. The need for peace and order is too insistent for that. But it will be crippled and its task made a great deal more difficult, for unsound, unstated reasons, which can find no home in any of the provisions of the Constitution.

The significance of the *Escobedo* case was its broadened interpretation of the Constitution concerning the Sixth Amendment protections for those accused of crimes. It extended the time frame during which suspects were entitled to have a lawyer present beyond the trial itself to the time of the interrogation. The decision was widely criticized by police officers who depended on confessions for evidence. It also raised many questions: it seemed to imply that suspects should be told of their right to remain silent and to have an attorney.

Name _____   Date _____

Escobedo v. Illinois (1964)

ELEMENTS OF THE CASE

Directions: Fill in the appropriate information for each of the following elements of this case.

1. State the issue before the Supreme Court in this case.

_____

_____

_____

_____

_____

2. What facts of the case were presented to the Court?

_____

_____

_____

_____

_____

3. What was the decision of the Court? What was the rationale behind it?

_____

_____

_____

_____

4. What was the effect of the decision?

_____

_____

_____

_____

Supreme Court Decision 16

Name _____ *Escobedo v. Illinois* (cont.)

Evaluation of the Case

Directions: Use your own judgment to evaluate the justices' decision
and state your opinion of that decision.

1. Do you agree with the majority who supported Escobedo or with the
    dissenting justices? Explain.

    _____

    _____

    _____

    _____

    _____

2. Do you think the *Escobedo* decision cripples law enforcement? Ex-
    plain.

    _____

    _____

    _____

    _____

    _____

3. Evaluate the following statement: *The task of the Court is to balance
    the rights of the individual with the needs of security for the society as
    a whole.* Do you think this case did so?

    _____

    _____

    _____

    _____

    _____

Supreme Court Decision 17

Miranda v. Arizona (1966)
Teacher Lesson Plan

Rationale

This lesson is designed to explore with students some of the changes in criminal procedure made under the Warren Court, specifically those that strengthened the constitutional protections (in the Sixth Amendment) for the rights of persons accused of crimes. This landmark Supreme Court decision required that suspects be read their rights, which has had a lasting effect on police procedure.

General Goals

This case study will provide students with opportunities to:

1. explore the challenges of American constitutional law
2. understand the processes and procedures of the judicial system
3. examine the role of the Supreme Court in the formation of public policy
4. explore the conflict between judicial activism and judicial restraint
5. examine the opinions of Supreme Court justices
6. demonstrate critical thinking skills

Directions

Student material is provided in four blackline masters on the following pages. These should be copied and distributed to students. They include a brief description of the *Miranda* case as well as questions for students to answer.

Elements of the Case presents questions to check student comprehension, providing an opportunity to review with students the central issues, the Court's decision and rationale, and the effects of the case.

Evaluation of the Case provides one or more critical thinking activities for students. In this section, students are asked to evaluate the case and express their own positions on its issues.

Answer Key and Extending the Lesson

An answer key for the questions is provided on the next page, along with suggested activities for extending the lesson.

Miranda v. Arizona (1966)

Answer Key

Elements of the Case

1. *Issue:* If police do not tell a suspect of his or her right to have an attorney present during questioning, can any statements made without an attorney be admitted into evidence or do they violate the Fifth Amendment right against self-incrimination?
2. Ernesto Miranda was arrested on a rape charge, taken into custody, identified by the victim, and questioned for two hours. He was not told he had the right to have an attorney present nor that he could remain silent. During the interrogation he confessed to the crimes and signed a written confession saying that the statement was given voluntarily and that he understood his rights. At the trial Miranda's attorney moved to suppress the evidence. Miranda was found guilty of kidnapping and rape and appealed on the basis of the Fifth Amendment protection against self-incrimination.
3. The Supreme Court declared that Miranda's confession was unlawfully obtained and so was not admissible as trial evidence. The case was sent back to the Arizona court, which could retry Miranda but without the evidence from his confession.
4. One result of this case was the "Miranda warnings," a specific set of procedural requirements to be followed in cases involving the questioning of a suspect in custody. The decision was controversial because of the limits it imposed on law enforcement officials.

Evaluation of the Case

1. Answers will vary, but students should try to dissociate themselves from distaste for Miranda and look at the ideas.
2. Answers should show that students have given careful consideration to the question of balancing efficient police work with constitutional rights.
3. Answers should show that students have given careful thought to the issue.

Extending the Lesson

1. Have students watch their favorite television police or crime dramas to see how the "Miranda warnings" have become part of standard police procedure. How are the warnings incorporated into the drama? Do the police officers portrayed in these dramas comment on the "Miranda warnings" positively or negatively?
2. Invite different officers of the court, such as a prosecutor, judge, defense attorney, or public defender, to visit your classroom and discuss the ramifications of the *Miranda* case from differing perspectives. You may also want to invite police representatives. If possible, organize a panel discussion in which students can ask questions of these people.
3. Have students read all the cases in this book concerning the 1960s decisions concerning the rights of the accused: *Gideon v. Wainwright, Escobedo v. Illinois, Miranda v. Arizona* (Decisions 15, 16, 17). The Warren Court was criticized by some for "protecting criminals." Have students debate whether they think the Court was defending individual rights or giving criminals too much leeway.

Miranda v. Arizona (1966)

Vocabulary

self-incrimination Giving testimony or other evidence that involves oneself in a crime and makes one subject to being prosecuted; protected against by the Fifth Amendment.

(writ of) habeas corpus Court order requiring that a person in custody be brought before a court so a judge can determine the legality of keeping him or her in jail.

counsel Legal advice or representation.

Reviewing the Case

In March 1963, Ernesto Miranda, an unemployed drifter who was mentally disturbed, was arrested by police in Phoenix, Arizona. He was charged with the kidnapping and rape of a young woman and was taken to the police station. In the police line-up, the young woman identified him as the person who had kidnapped and raped her. After the identification, Miranda was questioned for two hours by two Phoenix police officers. Both police officers testified in court that they had not told Miranda at any time that he had the right to have an attorney present.

After the questioning, the officers left the interrogation room with a signed confession. Above the confession was a paragraph stating that the suspect understood his rights and that the confession was given voluntarily.

At Miranda's trial, the statement was entered as evidence against him. Police officers testified that Miranda had confessed orally to the crime before giving the written confession. The defendant's attorney tried to have the confession ruled inadmissible, but the judge allowed the jury to hear the statement. Miranda was found guilty of both kidnapping and rape and sentenced to 20 to 30 years on both charges. The sentences were to be served concurrently [at the same time].

Miranda appealed his conviction to the Arizona State Supreme Court. He asked to have his conviction overturned on the grounds that the confession was obtained in violation of his Fifth Amendment protections against **self-incrimination**. The Fifth Amendment provides: "No person . . . shall be compelled in any criminal case to be witness against himself, nor be deprived of life, liberty, or property without due process of law. . . ."

The Arizona court, however, upheld the conviction. Miranda's attorney then filed for a writ of **habeas corpus**. The case went to the United States Supreme Court, which agreed to review the records of the case. The Court considered it along with three other cases, all dealing with using the statements of suspects who had been questioned in police custody without their lawyers present.

Two years earlier, in *Escobedo v. Illinois*, the Court had not allowed the admission of harmful evidence gained while interrogating Escobedo without his lawyer. Both the suspect and his lawyer had repeatedly asked that the attorney be present but had been refused until the questioning was finished. The Court had ruled that the evidence was obtained unlawfully, in violation of Escobedo's Sixth Amendment right to counsel. The decision had drawn criticism. Many, including four dissenting justices, had felt it would hamper police and prosecutors. The decision also left many law enforcement officers unsure of their obligations to advise suspects of their rights.

The issue before the Court: If police do not tell a suspect of his or her right to have an attorney present during questioning, can statements obtained be admitted into evidence or do they violate the Fifth Amendment right against self-incrimination?

The Court ruled 5–4 to overturn the decision of the Arizona court. It declared that Miranda's confession was unlawfully obtained and so was not admissible as trial evidence. The case was sent back to the Arizona court, which could retry Miranda but without the evidence from his confession.

Writing for the Court, Chief Justice Earl Warren spelled out some new limits:

The cases before us raise questions which go to the roots of our concepts of American criminal jurisprudence: the restraints society must observe consistent with the Federal Constitution in prosecuting individuals for crime. More specifically, we deal with the admissibility of statements obtained from an individual who is subjected to custodial police interrogation. . . .

The Court set up the following procedural safeguards:

1. Prior to questioning, a suspect must be advised of the right to remain silent.
2. Anything a suspect does say may be used against him or her in a court of law.
3. A suspect has a right to have an attorney present during questioning. The attorney may be of the suspect's choice or one retained by the government.
4. A suspect may waive the right to an attorney if desired, provided he or she does so voluntarily.
5. If a suspect wishes to have an attorney present, all questioning will cease until an attorney is present.
6. A suspect may at any time, even if the right to an attorney has been waived, refuse to answer any further questions without benefit of **counsel**.

Four justices dissented. Justice John Marshall Harlan wrote:

The new rules are not designed to guard against police brutality. . . . Those who use third-degree tactics and deny them in court are equally able and destined to lie as skillfully about warnings and waivers. Rather, the thrust of the new rules is to negate [destroy] all pressure, to reinforce the nervous or ignorant suspect, and ultimately to discourage any confession at all. . . .

In addition to his fears over the damage the rules would cause in eliminating confessions, Justice Harlan feared that the Court was putting society at risk with what he felt was a "hazardous experimentation."

Not surprisingly, the *Miranda* decision was controversial. Police departments all over the country ordered their officers to carry cards with the first four items of the above list printed on them. The warnings on these cards, which came to be known as the "Miranda Warnings," are read to suspects as they are placed in custody and before any questioning is lawfully allowed. Since the decision, the Court has chipped away at the ruling without overturning it. It has generally upheld it, however, in cases in which people have been convicted.

After the decision, Ernesto Miranda was retried in Arizona and convicted without the confession. After Miranda was paroled, he traveled around the southwestern United States autographing "Miranda Warnings" cards for the local police until he was stabbed to death in a quarrel over a card game.

Name _____   Date _____

Miranda v. Arizona (1966)

Elements of the Case

Directions: Fill in the appropriate information for each of the following elements of this case.

1. State the issue before the Supreme Court in this case.

_____

_____

_____

_____

2. What facts of the case were presented to the Court?

_____

_____

_____

_____

_____

3. What was the decision of the Court? What was the rationale behind it?

_____

_____

_____

_____

4. What was the effect of the decision?

_____

_____

_____

_____

Supreme Court Decision 17

Evaluation of the Case

Directions: Use your own judgment to evaluate the justices' decision and state your opinion of that decision.

1. In your opinion, was the majority or the dissent correct in this case? Explain.

_____

_____

_____

_____

_____

2. Do you think that the police should depend on confessions rather than using evidence? Explain.

_____

_____

_____

_____

3. Evaluate the following statement: *Society's failure to protect the rights of the guilty is society's failure to provide adequate protection of the rights of the innocent.* Do you agree or disagree with the statement? Explain.

_____

_____

_____

_____

_____

Supreme Court Decision 18

Schenck v. United States (1919)
Teacher Lesson Plan

Rationale

This lesson is designed to explore with students how historical situations have affected the Bill of Rights provisions protecting free speech. This Supreme Court decision, made during World War I, involved the question of sedition—open criticism of the government and its policies during a period of national crisis such as wartime. It established the well-known "clear and present danger" test.

General Goals

This case study will provide students with opportunities to:

1. explore the challenges of American constitutional law
2. understand the processes and procedures of the judicial system
3. examine the role of the Supreme Court in the formation of public policy
4. explore the conflict between judicial activism and judicial restraint
5. examine the opinions of Supreme Court justices
6. demonstrate critical thinking skills

Directions

Student material is provided in four blackline masters on the following pages. These should be copied and distributed to students. They include a brief description of *Schenck v. United States* as well as questions for students to answer.

Elements of the Case presents questions to check student comprehension, providing an opportunity to review with students the central issues, the Court's decision and rationale, and the effects of the case.

Evaluation of the Case provides one or more critical thinking activities for students. In this section, students are asked to evaluate the case and express their own positions on its issues.

Answer Key and Extending the Lesson

An answer key for the questions is provided on the next page, along with suggested activities for extending the lesson.

Schenck v. United States (1919)

Answer Key

Elements of the Case

1. *Issue:* Does the Espionage Act of 1917 violate the First Amendment with respect to Schenck's freedom of speech?
2. Schenck was accused of mailing circulars to approximately 15,000 U.S. Army draftees, encouraging them to resist the draft. The action was prohibited by one section of the Espionage Act of 1917. Schenck was convicted in district court. He asked the Supreme Court to overturn his conviction and declare the Espionage Act unconstitutional because it abridged the First Amendment guarantee of free speech.
3. The Supreme Court's decision upheld the lower court's conviction and declared that the Espionage Act was allowable in a wartime context. The Court acknowledged that Schenck might have been within his rights under other circumstances. But the effect of his speech presented a "clear and present danger" to army discipline and to the nation's ability to conduct the war. For these reasons, the Court declared Schenck's right to free speech could be limited.
4. It allowed for limitations on the individual's freedom of speech when balanced against wartime needs and public welfare. Justice Holmes created the "clear and present danger" test, which is still a guideline for balancing the needs of society with the rights of the individual.

Evaluation of the Case

1. Answers will vary, but students should give reasonable reasons for their opinions.
2. Answers will vary, but examples should show that students understand the meaning of the term.
3. Answers will vary. Some students may think that freedom of speech should never be limited; others will agree with the "clear and present danger" test.

Extending the Lesson

1. Have students research the Espionage Act and the other restrictive acts passed just before World War I and read excerpts from them in class. What do students think of the limits they place on free speech? Why did these acts seem necessary at the time?
2. Have students research the reasons why Congress established the draft (Selective Service) before the United States entered World War I. Be sure they are clear about the differences between volunteer armies and those based on a draft.
3. Have students compare the situation in this case with that of the *Pentagon Papers* case (Decision 19). Would the Pentagon Papers have been suppressed under the Espionage Act? Why or why not?

Schenck v. United States (1919)

Vocabulary

abridging Lessening, interfering with.

neutral Not allied with or supporting either side in a war or dispute.

draft To select people for required military service.

insubordination Unwillingness to accept orders from someone in authority.

affirm To agree or support, as when a higher court agrees with the earlier decision of a lower court.

Reviewing the Case

The First Amendment guarantee of free speech and expression reads: "Congress shall make no law . . . **abridging** the freedom of speech. . . ." But, at several different periods in the history of the United States, Congress has passed laws limiting how much citizens can criticize or resist government actions. Is this an abridgment of free speech? In the case of *Schenck v. United States*, the Supreme Court established a guideline that is still followed.

In 1917 the United States was still officially **neutral**, but its entry into World War I was imminent. To build up the army, Congress passed an act on May 18, 1917, that established a military **draft.** To encourage national unity in the war effort, Congress also passed several laws that limited criticism of the government and opposition to its policies. On June 15, 1917, Congress passed the Espionage Act. Sections of the Espionage Act prohibited any attempt to cause **insubordination** among military personnel or to interfere with the draft or with military recruitment.

Three days later Charles Schenck was arrested for violating the Espionage Act. He was accused of printing and mailing antiwar pamphlets to some 15,000 to 16,000 men who had been accepted for induction into the military under the Selective Service Act. Schenck was the general secretary of the American Socialist Party and, like most other members of the party, he strongly opposed the war. He claimed it was being fought for the benefit of Wall Street investors who would profit from the sale of merchandise to the military.

The U.S. District Court for Pennsylvania ruled that the pamphlets were designed to cause men to resist the draft. Therefore, the court decided, Schenck had violated the Espionage Act. Schenck claimed there was not enough evidence to convict him of the charges that had been brought against him. He said that his actions were a form of free speech and claimed that the Espionage Act abridged the rights of free speech. Thus, according to him, the act was unconstitutional. Convicted in the district court, Schenck appealed to the U.S. Supreme Court.

The issue before the Court: Does the Espionage Act violate the First Amendment in respect to Schenck's freedom of speech?

The Supreme Court ruled unanimously to **affirm** the decision of the district court against Schenck. Writing for the Court, Justice Oliver Wendell Holmes laid down a standard that would become famous:

> We admit that in many places and in ordinary times the defendants in saying all that was said in the circular would have been within their constitutional rights. But the character of every act depends on the circumstances in which it is done. The most stringent protection of free speech would not protect a man in falsely shouting fire in a theatre, and causing a panic. . . . The question in every case is whether the words used are used in such circumstances and are of such a nature as to create a clear and present danger that they will bring about the substantive [actual] evils that Congress has a right to prevent."

In the Schenck decision, the Supreme Court established clear limitations on freedom of speech. The guideline is the existence of a "clear and present danger," a situation in which free speech could bring harm to the general welfare. In such cases, Congress has the power to pass laws to protect its citizens and the national security of the United States even if those laws abridge free speech. The "clear and present danger" test is a way to balance the rights of the individual with those of society.

According to Justice Holmes, it made no difference that Schenck and the others had failed to interfere with military recruitment. ". . . We perceive no ground for saying that success alone warrants making the act a crime," he concluded.

Supreme Court Decision 18

Name _____   Date _____

Schenck v. United States (1919)

Elements of the Case

Directions: Fill in the appropriate information for each of the following elements of the case.

1. State the issue before the Court.

_____

_____

_____

_____

_____

2. What facts of the case were presented to the Court?

_____

_____

_____

_____

_____

3. What was the decision of the Court? What was the rationale behind it?

_____

_____

_____

_____

_____

4. What was the effect of the decision?

_____

_____

_____

_____

Evaluation of the Case

Directions: Use your own judgment to evaluate the justices' decision and state your opinion of that decision.

1. Do you agree that the free speech guarantees in the First Amendment should have limitations? Explain why you think as you do.

   _____

   _____

   _____

   _____

   _____

2. What does the term "clear and present danger" mean to you? Give at least two examples of such situations.

   _____

   _____

   _____

   _____

   _____

3. Does this ruling, in your opinion, strike a proper balance between the rights of the individual and the needs of society? Explain.

   _____

   _____

   _____

   _____

   _____

Supreme Court Decision 19

New York Times Co. v. United States (1971)
Teacher Lesson Plan

Rationale

This lesson is designed to explore with students some of the background to the Watergate scandal, including the early incidents surrounding the publication of the Pentagon Papers by *The New York Times* and *Washington Post*. This Supreme Court case also raised First Amendment issues of press freedom, prior censorship, and national security.

General Goals

This case study will provide students with opportunities to:

1. explore the challenges of American constitutional law
2. understand the processes and procedures of the judicial system
3. examine the role of the Supreme Court in the formation of public policy
4. explore the conflict between judicial activism and judicial restraint
5. examine the opinions of Supreme Court justices
6. demonstrate critical thinking skills

Directions

Student material is provided in four blackline masters on the following pages. These should be copied and distributed to students. They include a brief description of the *New York Times v. United States* case, known as the *Pentagon Papers* case, as well as questions for students to answer.

Elements of the Case presents questions to check student comprehension, providing an opportunity to review with students the central issues, the Court's decision and rationale, and the effects of the case.

Evaluation of the Case provides one or more critical thinking activities for students. In this section, students are asked to evaluate the case and express their own positions on its issues.

Answer Key and Extending the Lesson

An answer key for the questions is provided on the next page, along with suggested activities for extending the lesson.

New York Times Co. v. United States
(1971)

Answer Key

Elements of the Case

1. *Issue*: Can the U.S. government justify prior restraint of the publication of the Pentagon Papers or are the injunctions in violation of the First Amendment's protection of a free press?

2. Daniel Ellsberg stole classified Defense Department documents concerning the policy and conduct of American involvement in Southeast Asia. He turned them over to two newspapers, which began to publish them in a series of articles. The information in the documents was embarrassing to several administrations and pointed out that the government had lied on several occasions. Claiming the need for national security, the government sought injunctions to restrain the newspapers from publishing the information.

3. The Court disallowed the prior restraint of the publication by a 6-3 per curiam decision, agreeing with the Washington D.C. Court of Appeals and reversing the New York Court of Appeals. Each justice, however, wrote an opinion for or against the decision. The six justices supporting the decision found the prior restraint unjustified in its violation of a free press. The three dissenting justices thought that the speed and deviation from the normal Court process was unwise. They would have allowed the injunctions to remain in place until the evidence could be examined more thoroughly.

4. The publication was followed by a great distrust of the government and the creation of more antiwar sentiment. It did, however, reinforce the idea that the Court would look on prior restraint as unconstitutional unless the government could show an overriding need for this action.

Evaluation of the Case

1. Answers will vary, but students may simply agree generally with the majority or with the dissenting justices. Though not identical, the opinions on each side are similar.

2. Answers will vary and may depend on students' answers in question 1.

3. Answers should address the issue of doing the wrong thing for the right reasons and can be the basis for a discussion of various forms of civil disobedience.

Extending the Lesson

1. Have students use library microfilm to read *The New York Times* or *Washington Post* for the relevant period in June 1971. Have some students read the articles on the Pentagon study; have others analyze the press reaction to the government attempts to stop publication. If possible, have students read other newspaper reactions to this attempt at prior restraint (*The Boston Globe* and *St. Louis Post Dispatch* also became involved).

2. A number of books were published about this case and the events surrounding it. Have students read and report on some of them; one is *The Pentagon Papers: Secret History of the Vietnam War* by Neil Sheehan, et al. (1971).

New York Times Co. v. United States
(1971)

Vocabulary

Pentagon   Term for the U.S. Department of Defense or the military establishment in general (from the name of its building in Washington, D.C.).

injunction   A court order to cease or refrain from a particular action.

prior restraint   Government censorship of a work before it is printed or published.

per curiam   Latin for "by the court"; an unsigned or collectively authored opinion issued by the court.

precedent   An earlier court decision used as a guide or model in deciding similar cases.

Reviewing the Case

In the United States, the era of the Vietnam War was a time of sharp divisions and conflicts over both the conduct of the war and American involvement in it. In the spring of 1971, two of the country's major newspapers, *The New York Times* and the *Washington Post,* received copies of a secret Defense Department study of policy-making decisions concerning the conduct of the war. The source was Daniel Ellsberg, a former Defense Department employee.

Ellsberg, a veteran government official, knew that making secret documents public was against the law. The **Pentagon** study, however, showed that the government had lied about American involvement in Southeast Asia. Ellsberg wanted to expose these lies to the American people.

In June, both newspapers began to publish a series of articles based on the papers received from Ellsberg. The papers, which came to be known as the Pentagon Papers, contained important arguments concerning U.S. policy and the conduct of the war.

The federal government, represented by the Attorney General, asked the newspapers to stop publishing the papers on the grounds that they endangered national security. The newspapers refused. The government then moved to have the federal district courts in New York and in Washington, D.C., issue **injunctions.** A federal judge in New York issued a temporary injunction against publication, the first federal injunction ever issued to stop a newspaper from publishing.

A series of hearings, temporary injunctions, and appeals followed in the federal courts. The Court of Appeals for the District of Columbia lifted the injunction against the *Post.* In New York, the judge withdrew the injunction, but the appeals court restored it. The federal government quickly moved to have the U.S. Supreme Court review the cases together.

Ellsberg's actions were not the issue before the Court. Instead, the question was whether or not the government could justify **prior restraint** to prevent newspapers from publishing this information. Should the injunctions stand, or did they violate the First Amendment protections of the freedom of the press?

The case was argued on June 26, 1971, and the Court decided it four days later. The speed with which the Court issued the opinion showed the urgency of the case. But it also raised doubts. By a 6–3 vote the Court issued a **per curiam** opinion that prior restraint was not justified. The justices all wrote separate opinions.

Concurring with the majority, Justice Hugo Black wrote for himself and Justice Douglas:

I believe that every moment's continuance of the injunction against these newspapers amounts to a flagrant, indefensible, and continuing violation of the First Amendment.

Also in the majority, Justice William J. Brennan wrote:

Unless and until the Government has clearly made out its case, the First Amendment commands that no injunction may issue.

For himself and Justice White, Justice Potter Stewart wrote:

. . . I cannot say that disclosure . . . will result in direct, immediate, and irreparable damage to our Nation or its people. That being so, there can under the First Amendment be but one judicial resolution of the issue before us. I join the judgments of the Court.

The three dissenting justices also had a variety of opinions. Chief Justice Warren Burger wrote of his concern over the speed with which the Court had acted in this case:

As I see it, we have been forced to deal with litigation [legal questions] concerning rights of great magnitude without an adequate record, and surely without time for adequate treatment either in the prior proceedings or in this Court.

Burger would have left the injunction in place and ordered the district courts to proceed with the case in a slower, more deliberate fashion.

Justices John Marshall Harlan and Harry Blackmun concurred with Burger's dissenting opinion. Justice Harlan stated:

With all respect, I consider the Court has been almost irresponsibly feverish in dealing with these cases.

Justice Blackmun echoed these views:

The country would be none the worse off were the cases tried quickly, to be sure, but in the customary and properly deliberative manner.

Because U.S. action in Vietnam had proceeded through several administrations without an official declaration of war, there was no clear **precedent** for the Court to follow. In the World War I case of *Schenck v. United States* (1919), Congress had passed a law that clearly prohibited Schenck from interfering with the draft. In the Pentagon Papers case, the Court was required to decide between two conflicting forces: the right of the people to know and the right of the government to keep secrets in order to protect the nation. With this in mind, the significance of the case becomes clear.

The Supreme Court looks on government censorship of the press as a serious matter. Its decision meant that the government must prove its claims of national security before the press can be restrained from publishing information that the people otherwise have the right to know.

The newspapers were allowed to publish the articles in question. Readers were allowed to judge for themselves whether the government had acted properly in Vietnam. Many people, after reading the papers, strongly disapproved of the American presence in Vietnam, and the growing number of antiwar protesters increased. Depending on one's point of view, Ellsberg was either a hero or a traitor to the country. He was indicted for theft and espionage, but the judge ordered all charges dropped after it was found that FBI agents and White House officials had used illegal methods in looking for evidence against Ellsberg.

Name _____ Date _____

New York Times Co. v. United States
(1971)

Elements of the Case

Directions: Fill in the appropriate information for each of the following elements of this case.

1. State the issue before the Supreme Court in this case.

_____

_____

_____

_____

_____

2. What facts of the case were presented to the Court?

_____

_____

_____

_____

3. What was the decision of the Court? What was the rationale behind it?

_____

_____

_____

_____

4. What was the effect of the decision?

_____

_____

_____

_____

Supreme Court Decision 19

Name _____   *New York Times Co. v. United States*   (cont.)

Evaluation of the Case

Directions: Use your own judgment to evaluate the justices' decision
and state your opinion of that decision.

1. With which of the opinions did you agree? Explain.

_____

_____

_____

_____

_____

_____

2. Do you think the Court should have moved more slowly in this case?
   Explain.

_____

_____

_____

_____

_____

3. What is your opinion of Daniel Ellsberg in this case? Do you think his
   motives justified his violation of the law? Explain.

_____

_____

_____

_____

_____

Supreme Court Decision 19

Supreme Court Decision 20

United States v. Nixon (1974)
Teacher Lesson Plan

Rationale

This lesson is designed to explore with students some of the developments in the Watergate scandal. This Supreme Court case, part of the legal maneuvering that followed the Watergate break-in, questioned whether or not a President could invoke executive privilege to withhold evidence needed in a criminal trial. The case also raised questions about the principle of separation of powers.

General Goals

This case study will provide students with opportunities to:

1. explore the challenges of American constitutional law
2. understand the processes and procedures of the judicial system
3. examine the role of the Supreme Court in the formation of public policy
4. explore the conflict between judicial activism and judicial restraint
5. examine the opinions of Supreme Court justices
6. demonstrate critical thinking skills

Directions

Student material is provided in four blackline masters on the following pages. These should be copied and distributed to students. They include a brief description of the context of *United States v. Nixon* as well as questions for students to answer.

Elements of the Case presents questions to check student comprehension, providing an opportunity to review with students the central issues, the Court's decision and rationale, and the effects of the case.

Evaluation of the Case provides one or more critical thinking activities for students. In this section, students are asked to evaluate the case and express their own positions on its issues.

Answer Key and Extending the Lesson

An answer key for the questions is provided on the next page, along with suggested activities for extending the lesson.

United States v. Nixon (1974)

Answer Key

Elements of the Case

1. *Issue:* Can a district court order the President of the United States to turn over information he considers to be privileged information?
2. President Richard Nixon had in his possession tape recordings of conversations that the Watergate Special Prosecutor, Leon Jaworski, believed were needed in the trials of seven men charged with conspiracy in the Watergate cover-up. The district court issued a subpoena for the tapes. Nixon turned over edited transcripts of the tapes, alleging that an absolute right of executive privilege allowed the President, not the judiciary, the right to determine what could be released. The district court said that executive privilege and confidentiality were important but not absolute and that determining the law was the right of the judiciary.
3. The Court ruled to uphold the subpoena and require the President to supply the tapes as evidence. The specific needs of the courts to conduct a criminal trial outweighed the general use of privilege by the President. It agreed that executive privilege was important but subject to limitations, since the material on the tapes did not relate to national security or foreign affairs. It was the right of the courts to determine the law relating to that privilege.
4. The tapes were turned over to the district court and provided evidence in the trials. They also showed that President Nixon had also taken part in the criminal activities related to the Watergate break-in and cover-up. Under threat of impeachment proceedings, Nixon resigned from office on August 9, 1974. The case demonstrated that not even the President of the United States is above the law.

Evaluation of the Case

1. Although answers will vary, the only dissenters will be those who think a President should have the right to keep all matters confidential.
2. Answers should show that students have considered the question carefully; they may think that Presidents do have the right to keep secret certain matters of national security. Students are likely to think that this case was an abuse of executive privilege.
3. Answers should reflect students' understanding of the "checks and balances"—in particular between the executive branch and the judiciary; some may mention that Congress was also taking separate action in this case. The decision referred specifically to the first judicial review case, *Marbury v. Madison.*

Extending the Lesson

1. *All the President's Men*, by Bob Woodward and Carl Bernstein, two *Washington Post* reporters who played a large role in breaking the Watergate story, is a fascinating account of these events. Have some students read and report on the book. Alternatively, if time allows, obtain a videotape of the film version and show it to the class.
2. Many other Watergate personalities wrote their own accounts of these events, including White House staff members, the Watergate "plumbers," and Watergate special prosecutor Archibald Cox. Have students check the library to find what books are available, then choose one to read and review for the class.

United States v. Nixon (1974)

Vocabulary

grand jury Group of people who review the evidence against an accused person and decide whether it is sufficient to justify a criminal charge.

indictment Formal charge made by a grand jury when they believe there is sufficient evidence that a person has committed a crime.

subpoena Court order requiring a person to appear as a witness or supply testimony.

executive privilege Right of the President and other high officials of the executive branch to withhold information from Congress and from the courts.

Reviewing the Case

On March 1, 1974, a **grand jury** of the District Court for the District of Columbia issued **indictments** for seven men who were members of President Richard Nixon's White House staff and workers in his re-election campaign. They had been implicated in the cover-up of the previous summer's break-in at the Democratic National Committee headquarters in the Watergate building. The main charge against them was "conspiracy to obstruct justice." The charge also named President Nixon himself as an "unindicted co-conspirator" in the crimes.

The case marked a new stage in the ongoing events surrounding the Watergate break-in and the White House cover-up that followed. Earlier, the same grand jury had indicted the Watergate burglars themselves. Earlier investigations had revealed that presidential conversations with White House staff members during the past several years had been recorded on tape. These conversations were vital evidence in the trials of the seven accused conspirators. Nixon, however, said the tapes were in his personal custody.

In mid-April, Leon Jaworski, the special prosecutor handling the Watergate case, asked the district court to **subpoena** all tapes, papers, transcripts, and other writings that related to meetings between the President and others on specific dates concerned in the coming trial. This was the second set of tapes requested from the President in the course of the Watergate investigation.

On April 30, President Nixon released edited transcripts of the taped meetings in question but refused to turn over the originals or copies of the original tapes. His lawyers then moved that the court cancel the subpoena for any more material. They based their challenge on two grounds: **executive privilege** and the violation of separation of powers the subpoena represented.

Nixon's lawyers claimed that executive privilege was absolute. Therefore, no court had the right to order a President to release information—only the President himself could order the release of the material. The lawyers contended that if a President could not keep private the "confidential conversations" and other communications between himself and others, people would be reluctant to speak frankly about important matters. They did not argue that the tapes contained classified information or military secrets that would affect foreign policy or national security—merely that personal presidential conversations must be confidential or else the presidency itself would be weakened.

They also argued that the special prosecutor, appointed by the President, was part of the executive branch. Therefore, said the lawyers, the dispute was all within the executive branch. The courts did not have a role in it.

District Court Judge John Sirica rejected these arguments. He ruled that the President was required to comply with the subpoena and turn over the tapes. While the court agreed that executive privilege was valid, it said the privilege had limits. In fact, the U.S. Court of Appeals had earlier ruled against absolute presidential privilege regarding the tapes. Further, the court said, it was the judiciary's function to determine what the law was, not—as the President's case suggested—a right of the executive branch.

Nixon's attorneys appealed, and through a series of legal maneuvers, the case went to the U.S. Supreme Court. The issue before the Court: Can the district court order the President of the United States to turn over information he considers to be privileged information?

The Court ruled unanimously that the President had to turn over the tapes to District Court Judge John Sirica, who would review the material and rule on the admission of relevant information that would not endanger national security. Essentially the Court affirmed the original district court decision. It agreed that executive privilege was a necessary and vital tool of the President but noted it was not absolute. Referring to the landmark 1803 case of *Marbury v. Madison*, the Court repeated the ruling that it is "the province and duty of the judicial department to say what the law is."

That is, the President, as part of the executive branch, could not define the law relating to executive privilege. That was the job of the courts. No one, not even the President, was above the law. The Court also acknowledged that confidentiality was necessary but said that it too must give way to the rule of law. In this case, the evidence was necessary to ensure a fair trial for the Watergate defendants.

Chief Justice Warren Burger wrote the unanimous opinion of the Court:

A President's acknowledged need for confidentiality in the communications of his office is general in nature; whereas the constitutional need for production of relevant evidence in a criminal proceeding is specific and central to the fair adjudication [settlement] of a particular criminal case. . . . Without access to specific facts a criminal prosecution may be totally frustrated. The President's broad interest in confidentiality of communications will not be vitiated by disclosure of a limited number of conversations . . . shown to have some bearing on the pending criminal cases.

We conclude that when the ground for asserting privilege as to the subpoenaed materials sought for use in a criminal trial is based only on the generalized interest in confidentiality, it cannot prevail over the fundamental demands of due process of law in the fair administration of criminal justice. . . .

This decision had great consequences for the U.S. government: the Court ruled on July 24 that President Nixon was required to turn over the tapes. Within a few days, the House of Representatives began impeachment proceedings against Nixon, and on August 9, he resigned. The tapes had provided what many referred to as the "smoking gun"—clear proof that the President had not only known about the cover-up of criminal activities by his staff and supporters but had in fact ordered it. The evidence from the tapes helped convict those on trial.

Richard Nixon was the first President in history to resign the office. While many people hoped that he would be tried for crimes against the government, others feared such a trial would divide the country even further. Before any criminal charges were brought, President Gerald Ford, believing it would help the country return to normal more quickly, issued a presidential pardon to the former President.

Name _____   Date _____

United States v. Nixon (1974)

Elements of the Case

Directions: Fill in the appropriate information for each of the following elements of this case.

1. State the issue before the Supreme Court in this case.

_____

_____

_____

_____

_____

2. What facts of the case were presented to the Court?

_____

_____

_____

_____

_____

3. What was the decision of the Court? What was the rationale behind it?

_____

_____

_____

_____

_____

4. What was the effect of the decision?

_____

_____

_____

_____

Name _____

Evaluation of the Case

Directions: Use your own judgment to evaluate the justices' decision and state your opinion of that decision.

1. Do you agree with the Supreme Court's decision in this case? Or, should President Nixon have been allowed to keep the tapes secret? Explain.

_____

_____

_____

_____

2. What is your opinion of the concept of "executive privilege," which has evolved by custom, not law? How might a President abuse this privilege? Was this case an example?

_____

_____

_____

_____

3. What did this decision demonstrate about the separation of powers in American government? How did it reflect the principle of "judicial review"?

_____

_____

_____

_____

Supreme Court Decision 21

Baker v. Carr (1962)
Teacher Lesson Plan

Rationale

This lesson is designed to explore with students some of the influences exerted by the Warren Court through what are known as the Reapportionment Cases. This Supreme Court decision established the federal courts' willingness to take jurisdiction in assuring fair representation in state legislatures.

General Goals

This case study will provide students with opportunities to:

1. explore the challenges of American constitutional law
2. understand the processes and procedures of the judicial system
3. examine the role of the Supreme Court in the formation of public policy
4. explore the conflict between judicial activism and judicial restraint
5. examine the opinions of Supreme Court justices
6. demonstrate critical thinking skills

Directions

Student material is provided in four blackline masters on the following pages. These should be copied and distributed to students. They include a brief description of *Baker v. Carr* as well as questions for students to answer.

Elements of the Case presents questions to check student comprehension, providing an opportunity to review with students the central issues, the Court's decision and rationale, and the effects of the case.

Evaluation of the Case provides one or more critical thinking activities for students. In this section, students are asked to evaluate the case and express their own positions on its issues.

Answer Key and Extending the Lesson

An answer key for the questions is provided on the next page, along with suggested activities for extending the lesson.

Baker v. Carr (1962)

Answer Key

Elements of the Case

1. *Issues*: Does the 1901 Tennessee statute violate the constitutional rights of these voters? Can the federal courts take action on the constitutionality of a state statute apportioning state legislative seats?
2. In 1901, the state of Tennessee passed an apportionment act establishing state legislative districts. The act was not revised for more than 50 years, although population increased and shifted. Urban counties were particularly underrepresented in the legislature. The act conflicted with the state constitution, which required apportionment to be based on the U.S. census. A group of reform politicians and urban voters sued the state. A federal district court dismissed the case on the grounds that it was a political question that should be settled by legislators and that the federal courts had no jurisdiction.
3. The Supreme Court, by a 6–2 vote, determined that the case involved a constitutional right protected under the equal protection clause of the Fourteenth Amendment and, therefore, the district court did have jurisdiction. They reversed the ruling and ordered the case sent back to the lower court for action.
4. The ruling changed apportionment from a political question to a legal one in which federal courts, including the Supreme Court, had jurisdiction. This decision led to many other legal challenges to apportionment.

Evaluation of the Case

1. Answers will vary, but most students will recognize that the division of voting power was not fair as it existed at the time of the lawsuit.
2. Answers to this question can provide the basis for a discussion of federalism. For instance, is it the federal government's responsibility to assure all voters of an equal political voice, even in state and local government? This decision said it was.
3. Answers should show that students understand the concept of "equal protection under the law."

Extending the Lesson

1. Have students obtain a map of the legislative districts in your state and research current methods and standards for apportionment: How and by whom were the legislative lines drawn? Where are they drawn? When were they last changed? In doing this extension, you may want to explain the meaning and purposes of gerrymandering.
2. Have students compare the concerns of the plaintiffs in *Baker v. Carr* with the concerns of the states over apportionment at the Constitutional Convention in 1787. Does the makeup of the U.S. Senate follow the idea of "one person, one vote"? If not, how can it be justified?

Baker v. Carr (1962)

Vocabulary

apportionment The distribution of representatives among states or legislative districts.

injunction A court order to cease or refrain from a particular action.

reapportionment The redistribution of legislative seats among voting districts, usually because of changes in population.

at large Election system by which voters of a state or other region elect officials who represent the area as a whole, not separate districts.

jurisdiction Legal right of a court to act in a particular case.

justiciable Referring to something that is subject to legal or court action.

Reviewing the Case

In 1901, the Tennessee legislature passed an **apportionment** act that established voting districts and the number of representatives each district could elect to the two houses of the state legislature. For almost 60 years, there were no changes in this law or in the representation of different districts. During this time, however, the number of eligible voters in Tennessee grew from less than 500,000 to more than two million and the population shifted from rural areas to cities and suburbs.

In 1959, a group of reform politicians and urban voters, headed by Charles Baker, sued the state of Tennessee (represented by the secretary of state, Joe C. Carr). They asked the U.S. district court to declare the 1901 statute unconstitutional on the grounds that it violated the equal protection clause of the Fourteenth Amendment by debasing—reducing the value—of their votes. The suit also asked the District Court to issue an **injunction** to stop the state from holding any further elections under the old law. Until the legislature ordered **reapportionment**, Baker's group asked the court either to reapportion legislative seats based on a formula in the state constitution or to order new elec-

tions on an **at-large** basis. The standard in the Tennessee constitution was based on the number of qualified voters in each of the 95 counties.

Baker's lawsuit pointed out that the Tennessee legislature had not reapportioned since 1901, that population had changed drastically since that time, and that the structure of the state legislature made other approaches to reapportionment almost impossible. The suit also alleged that because of the present division of districts, about one-third of the state's voting population, if they lived in certain districts, could elect a majority of the 33 state senators and 99 state representatives. Voters in urban areas were particularly underrepresented. This meant that cities received less attention and less financial help from the state.

In some earlier cases, the U.S. Supreme Court had refused to hear reapportionment cases because they were "political questions." Now the U.S. district court dismissed Baker's case on the grounds that apportionment was the responsibility of the state legislature and not in the court's **jurisdiction.** The court acknowledged that the situation was a bad one. But it also believed that legislative reapportionment was a "political question," not a question for the courts.

Baker and the others then appealed the district court's ruling to the United States Supreme Court. The issues before the Court: Does the 1901 Tennessee statute violate the constitutional rights of these voters? Can the federal courts take action on the constitutionality of a state statute apportioning state legislative seats?

The Supreme Court ruled in a 6–2 vote that the denial of equal protection made the question a constitutional one. Under the Fourteenth Amendment, federal courts could act to protect that right. Justice William J. Brennan wrote for the majority:

We conclude that the complaint's allegations of a denial of equal protection present a **justiciable** constitutional cause of action upon which appellants are entitled to a trial and a decision. The right asserted is within the reach of judicial protection under the Fourteenth Amendment.

As for it being a political question, Brennan's majority opinion also pointed out, ". . . the mere fact that the suit seeks protection of a political right does not mean it presents a political question."

The majority of justices also agreed that the plaintiffs as legal voters had the right to challenge the Apportionment Act in district court, since the effects of the law harmed them and other voters in the counties where they lived. The decision was to send the case back to the district court for a new trial. Finding a remedy for the situation was left up to the lower court.

In *Baker v. Carr* the Court, for the first time, allowed federal courts to have jurisdiction in an apportionment case. This case opened the door for further suits concerning apportionment by removing it from the category of a political question and declaring it a legal issue guided by the Fourteenth Amendment.

Name _____ Date _____

Baker v. Carr (1962)

Elements of the Case

Directions: Fill in the appropriate information for each of the following elements of this case.

1. State the issue before the Supreme Court in this case.

_____

_____

_____

_____

_____

2. What facts of the case were presented to the Court?

_____

_____

_____

_____

3. What was the decision of the Court? What was the rationale behind it?

_____

_____

_____

_____

4. What was the effect of the decision?

_____

_____

_____

_____

Supreme Court Decision 21

Evaluation of the Case

Directions: Use your own judgment to evaluate the justices' decision and state your opinion of that decision.

1. In your opinion was the decision by the Court a proper one? Explain.

_____

_____

_____

_____

_____

2. Do you think it was proper for the federal courts to interfere in a matter concerning a state legislature? Why or why not?

_____

_____

_____

_____

_____

3. Look at the Fourteenth Amendment and explain in your own words why the Court decided that the equal protection clause had been violated.

_____

_____

_____

_____

_____

Supreme Court Decision 21

Supreme Court Decision 22

Wesberry v. Sanders (1964)
Teacher Lesson Plan

Rationale

This lesson is designed to explore with students some of the influences exerted by the Warren Court through what are known as the Reapportionment Cases. This Supreme Court case established the principle of "one person, one vote" by requiring congressional voting districts to be reapportioned so that members of the House of Representatives would represent relatively equal numbers of voters.

General Goals

This case study will provide students with opportunities to:

1. explore the challenges of American constitutional law
2. understand the processes and procedures of the judicial system
3. examine the role of the Supreme Court in the formation of public policy
4. explore the conflict between judicial activism and judicial restraint
5. examine the opinions of Supreme Court justices
6. demonstrate critical thinking skills

Directions

Student material is provided in four blackline masters on the following pages. These should be copied and distributed to students. They include a brief description of *Wesberry v. Sanders* as well as questions for students to answer.

Elements of the Case presents questions to check student comprehension, providing an opportunity to review with students the central issues, the Court's decision and rationale, and the effects of the case.

Evaluation of the Case provides one or more critical thinking activities for students. In this section, students are asked to evaluate the case and express their own positions on its issues.

Answer Key and Extending the Lesson

An answer key for the questions is provided on the next page, along with suggested activities for extending the lesson.

Wesberry v. Sanders (1964)

Answer Key

Elements of the Case

1. *Issue*: Does the Georgia statute deny equal representation in the U.S. House of Representatives to the residents of the Fifth Congressional District?

2. Wesberry and other voters in Georgia's Fifth Congressional District sued to change the Georgia law establishing district boundaries. The Fifth District had two to three times more people than other districts; its population was more than double the average number of people per district. The suit contended that the right to equal representation under Article I, Section 2, of the U.S. Constitution was being violated. The district court recognized the imbalance but dismissed the case on the grounds of jurisdiction. According to the court, apportionment was a political question and a state right. Plaintiffs then appealed to the Supreme Court.

3. The Supreme Court ruled 6-3 that Georgia's method of apportionment violated the Constitution. The majority interpreted the intent of the framers under Article I, Section 2, to mean that each person's vote should have approximately the same weight in electing the House of Representatives. They reversed the district court ruling.

4. The Court established its intention to participate in apportionment cases. The ruling set forth the principle of "one person, one vote" in drawing congressional districts. It led to many complaints about apportionment in other states and to widespread redistricting.

Evaluation of the Case

1. Answers will vary, depending on whether students think this was federal interference in state government or whether they think it was a proper remedy for unfair representation.

2. Answers should show that students have read this section thoughtfully. In *Wesberry*, the majority decided that the phrase "by the people of the several states" implied equal voting power.

3. Students should show that they understand that without such a decision, voters in underrepresented areas have less say in politics, while those in other districts have more power than their numbers warrant.

Extending the Lesson

1. Obtain a map of your state's congressional districts and have students research census statistics to see whether it complies with the "one person, one vote" principle. If there are imbalances, are they in rural or urban areas?

2. A third Reapportionment Case, *Reynolds v. Sims*, was decided shortly after *Wesberry* and *Baker v. Carr* (Decision 21 in this book). Assign a small group of students to research this Supreme Court decision and report to the class on how it carried out the "one person, one vote" principle.

3. Many states experienced changes in congressional representation after the 1990 census. Have students research whether your state gained or lost representatives or remained the same. If there were changes, how were the new district lines established?

Wesberry v. Sanders (1964)

Vocabulary

injunction A court order to cease or refrain from a particular action.

apportionment The distribution of representatives among states or legislative districts.

jurisdiction Legal right of a court to act in a particular case.

at large Election system by which voters of a state or other region elect officials who represent the area as a whole, not separate districts.

Reviewing the Case

The question of fair representation in Congress and in state legislatures has arisen in many states. In most cases, voters have believed that political maneuvering in drawing district lines has deprived them—as a group or as individuals—of an equal voice. In this case, James Wesberry and other voters of Fulton County, Georgia, charged that the apportionment of seats in the Georgia delegation to the United States House of Representatives violated their right to equal representation.

All the plaintiffs lived in Georgia's Fifth Congressional District, where Atlanta is located. According to the 1960 census, the district had 823,680 residents. The plaintiffs showed that this number was more than double the average number of people in the state's other congressional districts. The average population in the state's ten districts was 394,152. In fact, one district, the Ninth, had only 272,154 people. Since each district sent only one person to Congress, the representative for the Fifth District had to speak for two to three times more people than the representatives from other districts.

Wesberry and the others asked the U.S. District Court for the Northern District of Georgia to declare unconstitutional a 1931 act of the Georgia legislature, which had established the state's ten congressional districts. They said that the act violated Article I of the Constitution as well as the Fourteenth Amendment. They asked for an **injunction** restraining the Georgia governor and secretary of state from holding congressional elections in the state until the inequalities in **apportionment** between voting districts could be corrected.

State officials claimed that under the Constitution, apportionment was left up to the states. The district court agreed to dismiss the case, although it recognized that the Atlanta district was "grossly out of balance" with the others. Nevertheless, the court believed that federal courts had no **jurisdiction** because apportionment was a political question rather than a legal issue. It rejected *Baker v. Carr* as a precedent because the question there was state legislative districts, not congressional districts.

With the dismissal of the case in the district court, the plaintiffs appealed to the U.S. Supreme Court. The issue before the Court: Does the Georgia statute deny equal representation in the U.S. House of Representatives to the residents of the Fifth Congressional District?

The Supreme Court ruled 6–3 that Georgia's method of apportionment violated the Constitution and the intent of its framers under Article I, Section 2. According to the Court, the framers of the Constitution had provided that representatives to the lower house (the House of Representatives) be selected **at large** or by the creation of districts based on population. The choice of method was left up to each state's legislative body.

The Court ruled that if a state selected the district method, it assumed responsibility for ensuring that each vote counted equally in the selection of members of the House of Representatives. According to the Court the Constitution should be understood to mean that "as nearly as is practicable, one man's vote in a congressional election is to be worth as much as another's. . . ."

Writing the majority opinion for the Court, Justice Hugo Black continued:

No right is more precious in a free country than that of having a voice in the election of those who make the laws under which, as good citizens, we must live. Other rights, even the most basic, are illusory if the right to vote is undermined. Our Constitution leaves no room for classification of people in a way that unnecessarily abridges this right. . . . While it may not be possible to draw congressional districts with mathematical precision, that is no excuse for ignoring our Constitution's plain objective of making equal representation for equal numbers of people the fundamental goal for the House of Representatives. That is the high standard of justice and common sense which the founders set for us.

The dissenting justices thought that there was no constitutional basis for the "one person, one vote" idea. They also believed that the Constitution gave control of election matters to the states, with supervision by Congress, not the courts. Justice John Marshall Harlan also pointed out that under this rule, only 37 members of the House of Representatives were, at the time, legally elected.

Wesberry v. Sanders set forth the principle of "one person, one vote" in drawing congressional districts. It led to a number of other complaints about apportionment in other states and to widespread redistricting.

Name _____   Date _____

Wesberry v. Sanders (1964)

Elements of the Case

Directions: Fill in the appropriate information for each of the following elements of this case.

1. State the issue before the Supreme Court in this case.

_____

_____

_____

_____

_____

2. What facts of the case were presented to the Court?

_____

_____

_____

_____

_____

3. What was the decision of the Court? What was the rationale behind it?

_____

_____

_____

_____

_____

4. What was the effect of the decision?

_____

_____

_____

_____

_____

Supreme Court Decision 22

Evaluation of the Case

Directions: Use your own judgment to evaluate the justices' decision and state your opinion of that decision.

1. In your opinion, was the decision of the Court a proper one? Explain.

_____

_____

_____

_____

_____

2. Read Article I of the Constitution, particularly Sections 2 and 4. Explain in your own words what rules the Constitution makes for voting. Does anything in this Article justify "one person, one vote"? Where can you find justification for this idea?

_____

_____

_____

_____

_____

3. How does this opinion equalize the voting power of all citizens in electing and in being represented by members of Congress? Explain.

_____

_____

_____

_____

_____

Supreme Court Decision 23

Roe v. Wade (1973)
Teacher Lesson Plan

Rationale

This lesson is designed to explore with students the legal and social controversies surrounding a woman's right to end a pregnancy and the extent to which government can or cannot interfere with her decision. This landmark Supreme Court case legalized abortion within certain guidelines, beginning a nationwide debate on the issue.

General Goals

This case study will provide students with opportunities to:

1. explore the challenges of American constitutional law
2. understand the processes and procedures of the judicial system
3. examine the role of the Supreme Court in the formation of public policy
4. explore the conflict between judicial activism and judicial restraint
5. examine the opinions of Supreme Court justices
6. demonstrate critical thinking skills

Directions

Student material is provided in four blackline masters on the following pages. These should be copied and distributed to students. They include a brief description of *Roe v. Wade* as well as questions for students to answer.

Elements of the Case presents questions to check student comprehension, providing an opportunity to review with students the central issues, the Court's decision and rationale, and the effects of the case.

Evaluation of the Case provides one or more critical thinking activities for students. In this section, students are asked to evaluate the case and express their own positions on its issues.

Answer Key and Extending the Lesson

An answer key for the questions is provided on the next page, along with suggested activities for extending the lesson.

Roe v. Wade (1973)

Answer Key

Elements of the Case

1. *Issue:* Do laws barring abortion except in cases in which the pregnant woman's life is threatened violate the privacy rights of the Ninth and Fourteenth Amendments?
2. Jane Roe, a single pregnant woman in Dallas County, Texas, wished to have a safe, legal abortion performed under clean conditions in a clinic or hospital with licensed medical personnel. The state of Texas had a statute that made abortion a crime unless the pregnant woman's life was threatened. The district court declared the statute void on the grounds that it violated the privacy rights granted in the Ninth and Fourteenth Amendments, but dismissed a motion by Roe's attorney to issue an injunction forbidding the continued use of the statute. Both parties appealed the decision to the Supreme Court.
3. The Supreme Court affirmed the decision of the lower court to void the Texas statute, which it found too vague and broad. However it did not issue the injunction. In addition, the majority opinion established a set of conditions to guide the state's involvement in abortion procedures at various stages of pregnancy. The conditions allowed for increased regulation by the state as the pregnancy progressed.
4. The Court's decision was divisive and controversial, arousing political action by advocates on both sides of the abortion issue. Abortion became a political issue, affecting election outcomes and nominations for federal judgeships. With the appointment of conservative justices by Presidents Reagan and Bush, the Supreme Court has made several decisions weakening *Roe v. Wade.* These decisions have given states more leeway in passing laws regulating abortion and thus increased the pressure on individual state legislatures.

Evaluation of the Case

1. Answers will vary, as this is a controversial issue about which most students will have formed an opinion.
2. Answers will vary, depending on students' awareness of the current moves in the Supreme Court.
3. Answers will vary; students may point out that differing state laws might mean that a woman would have to travel to another place in order to have a legal abortion. Others may think that state laws would more accurately reflect statewide opinion.

Extending the Lesson

1. Have students research what your state laws on abortion were before the 1973 *Roe v. Wade* decision. Are there any laws on the books that were overruled by *Roe v. Wade*?
2. Have students do research to find out what important court cases have come about on the abortion issue since *Roe v. Wade.* Have them research the effects of these cases on your state's legislature. Have bills been introduced either to protect the right to choice or to place limits on access to abortion? Students may want to find out how legislators plan to vote if an abortion bill is proposed.

Roe v. Wade (1973)

Vocabulary

injunction A court order to cease or refrain from a particular action.

trimester A period of three months.

Reviewing the Case

In 1970, Jane Roe, a woman living in Dallas County, Texas, asked the U.S. District Court for the Northern District of Texas to declare unconstitutional the Texas statutes outlawing abortion. The name *Jane Roe* was used to protect her privacy. Roe, a pregnant single woman, had hoped to terminate her pregnancy with the assistance of qualified, licensed medical personnel in the clean, safe conditions of a clinical setting. Texas laws, however, made abortion a crime except when performed to preserve the life of the mother. Roe could not afford to travel to another state for the procedure.

In her suit, Roe asked the district court not only to declare the statutes unconstitutional but also to issue an **injunction** barring the state from applying the statutes. She claimed that the Texas laws violated her constitutional rights under the First, Fourth, Fifth, Ninth, and Fourteenth Amendments.

The district court did declare the statutes void, saying they were vague and so broad that they infringed on Roe's constitutional rights of privacy. The court noted that the "fundamental right of single women and married persons to choose whether to have children is protected by the Ninth Amendment, through the Fourteenth Amendment. . . ." The court did not issue the injunction, however. Roe appealed the decision concerning the injunction to the U.S. Supreme Court. Henry Wade, district attorney for Dallas County, cross-appealed the decision to void the statute.

The issue before the Court: Do laws barring abortion except in cases in which the pregnant woman's life is threatened violate the privacy rights of the Ninth and Fourteenth Amendments?

The Supreme Court, in a 6–3 decision, ruled that the Texas statutes were unconstitutional because they were too broad and made no distinction between early and late abortions. It believed that Roe's privacy rights had been violated but that these rights were limited. Believing that the decision itself prohibited the Texas laws from being applied, the Court did not order an injunction.

Justice Harry Blackmun, who wrote the majority opinion, began with a lengthy review of the history of abortion legislation and attitudes toward it. He noted that restrictive state laws making abortion a crime dated mainly from the late 19th century. The conclusion of the majority of the Court was a compromise between a woman's right to privacy and the state's interest in regulating medical practice and protecting prenatal life.

Basic to the decision was the Court's view of privacy. Justice Blackmun wrote:

This right of privacy, whether it be founded in the Fourteenth Amendment's concept of personal liberty and restrictions upon state action, as we feel it is, or, as the District Court determined, in the Ninth Amendment's reservation of rights to the people, is broad enough to encompass a woman's decision whether or not to terminate her pregnancy. The detriment that the state [of Texas] would impose upon the pregnant woman by denying this choice altogether is apparent. . . .

We therefore conclude that the right of personal privacy includes the abortion decision, but that this right is not unqualified and must be considered against important state interests in regulation. . . .

One premise of the Texas statute was that life begins at the moment of conception. Believing that it is the duty of the state to protect life, Texas had banned abortion. The Court, however, would not take a position on the question of when life begins. Blackmun pointed out that neither religion, medicine, nor philosophy could agree on an answer. He did review briefly what he termed "the wide divergence of thinking on this most sensitive and difficult question. . . ."

Even without answering the question of when life begins, the Court believed that the state did, at some point, have a legitimate interest in both the health of the mother and the well-being of "potential life." It therefore established time guidelines for the states, based on the concept of viability. The Court defined viability as the point at which a fetus can have "meaningful life outside the mother's womb." It divided the normal nine months of pregnancy into three **trimesters**:

For approximately the first trimester, the abortion decision is the exclusive right of the woman and her physician. From approximately the end of the first trimester, the state may, if it chooses, regulate abortions "in ways that are reasonably related to maternal health." The state may, for instance, regulate where abortions can be performed—hospitals, clinics, etc. (This second stage approximates the second trimester.)

Finally, from the point of viability (a period generally including most or all of the last trimester), the Court guidelines gave the state much more power. It could regulate and even prohibit abortion except when it was considered medically necessary to preserve the mother's life or health.

Justice William Rehnquist strongly disagreed with the decision. Writing in dissent, he said:

I have difficulty in concluding, as the Court does, that the right of "privacy" is involved in this case.

Roe v. Wade was one of the most controversial and divisive decisions ever handed down by the Supreme Court. Few other cases have generated as much emotion or action on the part of the American people. Groups for and against the right to choose abortion have solidified into powerful political forces. Both sides have demonstrated publicly. Since the *Roe* decision, some candidates for elected office have been judged on the basis of their positions on abortion. Judges appointed to the federal courts have had their positions on abortion used as the basis for challenging their qualifications. Both the Reagan and Bush administrations took positions against the right to choose and acted through executive orders and appointments to make legal abortions more difficult to obtain.

With the appointment of a number of justices by Presidents Reagan and Bush, the Supreme Court has altered its approach to the abortion question. A number of later decisions have weakened the provisions of *Roe v. Wade,* allowing state legislatures more leeway in passing restrictive statutes concerning many aspects of abortion.

Name _____ Date _____

Roe v. Wade (1973)

Elements of the Case

Directions: Fill in the appropriate information for each of the follow-ing elements of this case.

1. State the issue before the Supreme Court in this case.

_____

_____

_____

_____

_____

2. What facts of the case were presented to the Court?

_____

_____

_____

_____

3. What was the decision of the Court? What was the rationale behind it?

_____

_____

_____

_____

_____

4. What was the effect of the decision?

_____

_____

_____

_____

Supreme Court Decision 23

Evaluation of the Case

Directions: Use your own judgment to evaluate the justices' decision and state your opinion of that decision.

1. If you were a Supreme Court justice, what would your decision have been in this case? Explain.

_____

_____

_____

_____

_____

_____

2. Do you think the decision in *Roe v. Wade* will be overturned? Explain your reasoning.

_____

_____

_____

_____

_____

_____

3. Overturning *Roe v. Wade* would return the question of abortion to individual state legislatures. Do you think this is a good idea or not?

_____

_____

_____

_____

_____

_____

Supreme Court Decision 24

Webster v. Reproductive Health Services (1989)
Teacher Lesson Plan

Rationale

This lesson is designed to explore with students the legal and social controversies surrounding a woman's right to end a pregnancy and the extent to which government can or cannot interfere with her decision. This Supreme Court case marked the Court's reconsideration of its landmark 1973 decision legalizing abortion within certain guidelines.

General Goals

This case study will provide students with opportunities to:

1. explore the challenges of American constitutional law
2. understand the processes and procedures of the judicial system
3. examine the role of the Supreme Court in the formation of public policy
4. explore the conflict between judicial activism and judicial restraint
5. examine the opinions of Supreme Court justices
6. demonstrate critical thinking skills

Directions

Student material is provided in four blackline masters on the following pages. These should be copied and distributed to students. They include a brief description of the *Webster* case as well as questions for students to answer.

Elements of the Case presents questions to check student comprehension, providing an opportunity to review with students the central issues, the Court's decision and rationale, and the effects of the case.

Evaluation of the Case provides one or more critical thinking activities for students. In this section, students are asked to evaluate the case and express their own positions on its issues.

Answer Key and Extending the Lesson

An answer key for the questions is provided on the next page, along with suggested activities for extending the lesson.

Webster v. Reproductive
Health Services (1989)

Answer Key

Elements of the Case

1. *Issue*: Do the challenged provisions of the Missouri statute violate the Constitution? Should *Roe v. Wade* be overturned?
2. In 1986 the Missouri legislature passed a law placing new restrictions on abortion procedures in the state. Five health care professionals, including a St. Louis family planning and abortion clinic called Reproductive Health Services, brought suit in district court. They charged that the law was unconstitutional on the grounds that it violated a woman's right to privacy outlined in *Roe v. Wade*. The District Court found the Missouri law unconstitutional; the appeals court upheld the decision. State Attorney General William Webster appealed to the U.S. Supreme Court.
3. The Court was deeply divided. It ruled 5-4 to overturn the lower court on the issue of state funding for abortion and on the constitutionality of viability testing. It did not rule on the preamble or the prohibition of state funds for counseling women to have abortions. Although the majority justices had many different reasons for their opinions, they made their ruling within the boundaries of *Roe v. Wade* and did not choose to reconsider it. The dissenting justices feared for the survival of the protections that *Roe v. Wade* had given women for sixteen years.
4. The *Webster* decision was seen as a serious setback for pro-choice forces and a victory for the anti-abortion groups who wanted to overturn *Roe v. Wade*. It showed that the Court was willing to allow states much more leeway in restricting abortion. This made the issue one for the state legislatures more than for the courts. The decision also made it clear that several justices were ready to overturn *Roe v. Wade* when the appropriate case came along.

Evaluation of the Case

1. Answers will vary, although students may realize that the general slant of the justices was opposed to the earlier decision.
2. Answers will vary, depending mainly on students' own opinions on the issue.
3. Answers should show students recognize that counseling and medical advice may be protected by the First Amendment, regardless of legal decisions regarding abortion.

Extending the Lesson

1. The right to choose an abortion is a controversial and emotional issue. Rather than debating the abortion issue itself in class, you may want to have students research what, if any, abortion legislation is being considered in your state legislature. What are the current laws affecting abortion and family planning issues? Are any of them in conflict with *Roe v. Wade*?

   Alternatively, have students review what part the abortion debate is playing in state or local elections.
2. If students have not read the lesson on *Roe v. Wade*, have them do so (Decision 23 in this book). Have them discuss the effects of *Webster* on *Roe v. Wade*.

Webster v. Reproductive Health Services (1989)

Vocabulary

viability The point in a pregnancy at which a human fetus is capable of surviving outside the mother's body with or without medical aid.

injunction A court order to cease or refrain from a particular action.

trimester A period of three months.

Reviewing the Case

In 1986, the Missouri legislature passed an act to change and strengthen the existing state statutes governing abortion. There were four points in the act that would be challenged in court. The new law began with an introduction, or preamble, stating that the "life of each human being begins at conception." One provision of the act required Missouri laws to be interpreted to give the unborn all the legal and constitutional rights of other persons. The new law also prohibited public funding of abortion counseling and the use of public facilities (such as public hospitals) for abortions. Finally, the act required physicians to conduct tests of **viability** before performing an abortion after the 20th week of pregnancy.

Shortly after the act was passed, five health care professionals filed a lawsuit challenging the act's constitutionality under the First, Fourth, Ninth, and Fourteenth Amendments. They alleged that the law violated a number of rights, including a woman's right to privacy and the right to practice medicine. They asked for an **injunction** to prevent the state from enforcing the law. One of the groups represented was Reproductive Health Services, a St. Louis clinic for family planning and abortion services.

The district court for western Missouri agreed that several provisions of the act were unconstitutional and issued a restraining order to prevent their enforcement. On appeal, the Eighth Circuit Court of Appeals affirmed this decision. Both rulings referred to the

1973 Supreme Court decision in *Roe v. Wade*. The state of Missouri, represented by its attorney general, William Webster, appealed to the U.S. Supreme Court.

According to the 1973 landmark decision in *Roe v. Wade*, a woman's right to have an abortion was protected under the constitutional right to privacy. The Court had also ruled, however, that the state had an interest in regulating medical procedures and protecting potential life after viability. For these reasons, the Court had set some guidelines and limitations, based generally on **trimester** divisions. Early in the pregnancy, the decision remained wholly with a woman and her doctor. Later, the state could regulate medical surroundings. In the third trimester, after presumed viability, the state could regulate or prohibit abortion itself.

The issue now before the Court: Do the challenged provisions of the Missouri statute violate the Constitution? Should *Roe v. Wade* be overturned?

A sharply divided Supreme Court ruled by a 5–4 vote to uphold certain parts of the Missouri law. It stopped short of reconsidering *Roe* itself, although the opinion made it clear that several justices were ready to modify and narrow that decision. The Court did not address all four crucial points in the Missouri law, nor did all the justices in the majority support the entire decision.

The Court's decision upheld Missouri's ban on the use of public facilities (such as hospitals) for abortions and on allowing public employees to perform the procedure. The Court's ruling also allowed the state to require viability testing, an expensive process, after the 20th week of pregnancy before permitting an abortion.

The Court did not rule on the other two issues. One was the controversial preamble regarding the point at which life begins. The other concerned the right to give abortion counseling.

The majority opinion, written by Justice

William Rehnquist, was critical of many parts of *Roe*. According to the opinion, viability testing did not violate a woman's right to an abortion but only allowed a doctor to perform a test. This procedure was justified, the Court said, because the state did have an interest in potential life throughout the entire pregnancy. This opinion was contrary to the guidelines set down in *Roe,* which did not allow state interference early in a pregnancy.

The opinion also said that prohibiting state funding for abortion did not impair a woman's right to have the procedure; it merely let the state refuse to pay for it through public assistance or public clinics. The Court did not rule on the question of using public funds for counseling about abortion.

Justices Byron White and Anthony Kennedy joined in most of Rehnquist's opinion. Justice Antonin Scalia, though he voted with the majority, would have gone further and overturned *Roe v. Wade* outright. Scalia wrote that not to overturn *Roe* in this case was delaying the inevitable. He believed that the Constitution did not support the right to privacy.

Justice Sandra Day O'Connor, who also voted in the majority, did not think that this was the time to reconsider *Roe v. Wade*. She did not find the Missouri law unconstitutional or in conflict with *Roe*.

On the other hand, the dissenting justices all strongly upheld *Roe*. Justice Harry Blackmun, who wrote the opinion in *Roe*, wrote for his fellow Justices Brennan and Marshall:

Today, *Roe v. Wade*, and the fundamental constitutional right of women to decide whether to terminate a pregnancy, *survive but are not secure.* . . . Although today, no less than yesterday, the Constitution and the decisions of this Court prohibit a State from enacting laws that inhibit women from the meaningful exercise of that right, a plurality of this Court implicitly invites every state legislature to enact more and more restrictive abortion regulations in order to provoke more and more test cases. . . .

The dissenting justices believed that the majority justices had disregarded the provisions of *Roe* without actually confronting it. They also believed that the justices had betrayed women who counted on the protections given by *Roe v. Wade*.

Justice Potter Stewart, one of the dissenting justices, also wrote a separate dissent. He believed that the preamble to the Missouri law violated the First Amendment ban on state support of religious views. The Court had ruled that the law's statement that life begins at conception was nothing more than a value judgment by the state of Missouri.

The *Webster* decision was seen as a serious setback for pro-choice forces and a victory for the anti-abortion groups who wanted to overturn *Roe v. Wade*. It showed that the Court was willing to allow states more leeway in restricting abortion. This made the issue one for the legislatures more than for the courts.

Several majority justices left little doubt that they would vote to overturn *Roe v. Wade* if the proper case came to the Court. Most reasoned that abortion was never intended to be protected as a fundamental privacy right. They would leave the question to the states to decide.

Name _____ Date _____

Webster v. Reproductive Health Services (1989)

Elements of the Case

Directions: Fill in the appropriate information for each of the following elements of this case.

1. State the issue before the Supreme Court in this case.

_____

_____

_____

_____

_____

2. What facts of the case were presented to the Court?

_____

_____

_____

_____

_____

_____

3. What was the decision of the Court? What was the rationale behind it?

_____

_____

_____

_____

4. What was the effect of the decision?

_____

_____

_____

_____

Supreme Court Decision 24

Name _____   *Webster v. Reproductive Health Services* (cont.)

Evaluation of the Case

Directions: Use your own judgment to evaluate the justices' decision and state your opinion of that decision.

1. How do you think this decision affected *Roe v. Wade?* Explain.

_____

_____

_____

_____

2. Pro-choice advocates feel this decision put an unfair burden on poor women, since it allowed states to prohibit the use of public funds for abortions or giving information about abortion. Do you agree or disagree? Explain.

_____

_____

_____

_____

3. One of the issues in abortion is the kind of information and counseling that clinics can give women who ask about abortion. From what you know about Americans' constitutional rights, do you think the government can regulate what doctors or other health care professionals tell their patients?

_____

_____

_____

_____

Supreme Court Decision 25

Schechter Poultry Corp. v. United States (1935)
Teacher Lesson Plan

Rationale

This lesson is designed to explore with students the conflicts between the courts and the executive branch regarding many New Deal statutes and programs. This Supreme Court case specifically questioned the constitutionality of the National Industrial Recovery Act.

General Goals

This case study will provide students with opportunities to:

1. explore the challenges of American constitutional law
2. understand the processes and procedures of the judicial system
3. examine the role of the Supreme Court in the formation of public policy
4. explore the conflict between judicial activism and judicial restraint
5. examine the opinions of Supreme Court justices
6. demonstrate critical thinking skills

Directions

Student material is provided in four blackline masters on the following pages. These should be copied and distributed to students. They include a brief description of the *Schechter* case as well as questions for students to answer.

Elements of the Case presents questions to check student comprehension, providing an opportunity to review with students the central issues, the Court's decision and rationale, and the effects of the case.

Evaluation of the Case provides one or more critical thinking activities for students. In this section, students are asked to evaluate the case and express their own positions on its issues.

Answer Key and Extending the Lesson

An answer key for the questions is provided on the next page, along with suggested activities for extending the lesson.

Schechter Poultry Corp.
v. United States (1935)

Answer Key

Elements of the Case

1. *Issues:* Can Congress delegate its legislative power to allow the President power over industry codes? Can Congress regulate this poultry company as part of its power over interstate commerce?
2. The National Industry Recovery Act was designed to encourage industrial recovery during the Depression by setting up industry codes that were to be approved by presidential executive order. The Schechter brothers, owners of the Schechter Poultry Corporation in New York City, were charged and convicted of violating the Live Poultry Codes. They charged that the codes were unconstitutional.
3. The Court unanimously ruled the codes were an unwarranted delegation of lawmaking power to the President. It further ruled that Congress had no constitutional authority to regulate the Schechters' poultry company because it was no longer in interstate commerce; the company was active only within New York State.
4. The decision ruled the National Industrial Recovery Act unconstitutional. Along with several other Court rulings against New Deal legislation, this decision worsened relations between the President and the Court. These decisions increased Roosevelt's determination to alter the makeup of the Supreme Court. After 1937, however, the Supreme Court changed its attitude and began to support some New Deal programs.

Evaluation of the Case

1. Answers will vary, depending on whether students think the NRA codes were helpful to industry.
2. Answers should show that students understand the principle of separation of powers; Congress should have set down laws that the President carried out, rather than letting the President make laws.
3. Answers will vary, depending on students' knowledge of the controversy over the growing powers of the President. Students may suggest that such powers would be given in wartime; some may think that the Depression did warrant them.

Extending the Lesson

1. Have students research the New Deal with respect to President Roosevelt's method of dealing with the Depression compared with that of President Hoover. Have them compare each President's (a) attitude toward government involvement in providing solutions and (b) programs for solving the problems.
2. Have small groups research and report on the work, achievements, and failures of other major New Deal programs, such as the WPA and CCC.

Schechter Poultry Corp. v. United States (1935)

Vocabulary

executive order A regulation or order issued by the President to enforce a treaty or law; it does not require congressional approval but has the force of law.

interstate commerce The transaction of business or trade across state lines, as opposed to business transacted within one state.

Reviewing the Case

To overcome the hardships of the Great Depression, Franklin D. Roosevelt promised to use the weight of the national government to remedy the country's problems. After his election as President in 1932, he brought in a sweeping program of changes that became known as the New Deal. Its programs aimed at relief for the poor and unemployed, economic recovery, and reforms in the economic structure.

Some New Deal legislation was aimed at helping specific sectors of the economy recover from the Depression. One major program was the National Industrial Recovery Act which created the National Recovery Administration, usually called the "NRA." The act gave considerable power to the executive branch. It asked each area of industry to set up codes of fair competition that would be approved by the President by **executive order**. The code for a given industry might include, for example, wage and price scales, limits on working hours, and restrictions on certain trade practices. The purpose of the codes was to ensure that fair competition would exist in all areas so that all businesses would be able to recover. There were both civil and criminal penalties for ignoring the codes.

The NRA encountered opposition and problems. Some critics felt the restrictions hindered recovery rather than helping it. Some found the regulations burdensome and ignored them.

Among those who ignored the law were the Schechter brothers, who were poultry dealers in New York City. Their company, A.L. Schechter Poultry Corp., bought live poultry shipped in from various states for sale in New York City. The Schechters purchased, slaughtered, and sold their product within the city of New York. They disregarded the codes of fair competition in order to sell below the price of their competitors and increase their profits.

The company was charged and convicted in the district court in New York on eighteen counts of violating the NRA Live Poultry Code. The Schechters had violated the code for hours and wages: a maximum of 40 hours a week, a minimum of 50 cents an hour. They had also violated the code on selling practices, filing reports, and even selling diseased and uninspected chickens. This last violation gave the case the popular nickname of the "Sick Chicken Case."

The Schechters appealed their conviction to the circuit court of appeals. They argued that the NRA codes amounted to delegation of legislative power by Congress. They also said that their business took place within New York and so was not subject to the rules for **interstate commerce**. The court of appeals upheld all the charges except the violation of wages and working hours. Both sides appealed the case to the United States Supreme Court.

The issues before the Court: Can Congress delegate its legislative power to allow the President power over industry codes? Can Congress regulate this poultry company as part of its power over interstate commerce?

The Supreme Court essentially said "no" to both questions. It overturned all the lower court convictions. The justices ruled unanimously that Congress could not constitutionally delegate such extensive lawmaking powers to the executive branch. Congress had also given too much legislative freedom to the industry associations that made up the codes. The Court said that Congress should have set up more detailed standards for industries. Under this part of the decision, the NRA system of industry codes was unconstitutional. Even justices who supported other New Deal legislation voted against the NRA. Writing for the entire Court, Chief Justice Charles Evans Hughes said:

Extraordinary conditions may call for extraordinary remedies. But the argument necessarily stops short of an attempt to justify action which lies outside the sphere of constitutional authority. Extraordinary conditions do not create or enlarge constitutional power. The Constitution established a national government with powers deemed to be adequate, as they have proved to be in both war and peace, but these powers of the national government are limited by the constitutional grants. Those who act under these grants are not at liberty to transcend the imposed limits because they believe that different power is necessary.

The Court further ruled that the company's business activity did not fall under the authority of Congress's authority to regulate interstate commerce. Although the chickens were shipped from different states, the Schechters purchased, processed, and sold them within New York State. As the Court put it, the chickens "had come to a permanent rest within the state." They were no longer part of interstate commerce. Chief Justice

Hughes explained what the justices found to be specifically wrong with the NRA:

. . . Paragraph 3 of the Recovery Act is without precedent. It supplies no standards for any trade, industry or activity. . . . Instead of prescribing rules of conduct, it authorizes the making of codes to prescribe them. . . . In view of the scope of that broad declaration, and of the nature of the few restrictions that are imposed, the discretion of the President in approving or prescribing codes, and thus enacting laws for the government of trade and industry throughout the country, is virtually unfettered. We think that the code-making authority thus conferred is an unconstitutional delegation of legislative power.

The result of this decision was to declare the entire National Industrial Recovery Act unconstitutional. On the same day as the Schechter decision, the Court also found two other New Deal measures unconstitutional. A few days later, President Franklin D. Roosevelt attacked the Court's "horse and buggy" interpretation of the Constitution.

The decision worsened relations between the President and the Court, which also overturned several other pieces of New Deal legislation in the following year. These decisions increased Roosevelt's determination to alter the makeup of the Supreme Court. After 1937, however, the Supreme Court changed its attitude and began to support some New Deal programs.

Name _____   Date _____

Schechter Poultry Corp.
v. United States (1935)

Elements of the Case

Directions: Fill in the appropriate information for each of the following elements of this case.

1. State the issue before the Supreme Court in this case.

_____

_____

_____

_____

2. What facts of the case were presented to the Court?

_____

_____

_____

_____

3. What was the decision of the Court? What was the rationale behind it?

_____

_____

_____

_____

4. What was the effect of the decision?

_____

_____

_____

_____

Name _____ *Schechter Poultry Corp. v. United States* (cont.)

Evaluation of the Case

Directions: Use your own judgment to evaluate the justices' decision and state your opinion of that decision.

1. Do you think the Court made the proper decision in this case? Explain.

_____
_____
_____
_____
_____

2. Why was Congress not allowed to delegate such broad law-making powers to the President? How does the principle of "separation of powers" apply? Explain.

_____
_____
_____
_____
_____

3. Do you think there are any circumstances under which the Court would have allowed Congress to give the President such great law-making power? Explain.

_____
_____
_____
_____
_____

Supreme Court Decision 25

Supreme Court Decision 26

United States v. Butler (1936)
Teacher Lesson Plan

Rationale

This lesson is designed to explore with students the conflicts between the courts and the executive branch regarding much New Deal legislation. This Supreme Court case specifically involved the constitutionality of the processing tax imposed as part of the Agricultural Adjustment Act (1933).

General Goals

This case study will provide students with opportunities to:

1. explore the challenges of American constitutional law
2. understand the processes and procedures of the judicial system
3. examine the role of the Supreme Court in the formation of public policy
4. explore the conflict between judicial activism and judicial restraint
5. examine the opinions of Supreme Court justices
6. demonstrate critical thinking skills

Directions

Student material is provided in four blackline masters on the following pages. These should be copied and distributed to students. They include a brief description of the *Butler* case as well as questions for students to answer.

Elements of the Case presents questions to check student comprehension, providing an opportunity to review with students the central issues, the Court's decision and rationale, and the effects of the case.

Evaluation of the Case provides one or more critical thinking activities for students. In this section, students are asked to evaluate the case and express their own positions on its issues.

Answer Key and Extending the Lesson

An answer key for the questions is provided on the next page, along with suggested activities for extending the lesson.

United States v. Butler (1936)

Answer Key

Elements of the Case

1. *Issue:* Is the Agricultural Adjustment Act a constitutional use of the congressional power to tax?
2. The Agricultural Adjustment Act authorized the Secretary of Agriculture to levy a tax on agricultural processors in order to pay crop reduction benefits to farmers. The goal was to reduce farm production and thus raise farm prices. Butler and other receivers of Hoosac Mills challenged the act, saying that the tax on processors of cotton was an unconstitutional use of Congress's taxing powers to regulate agriculture.
3. The Supreme Court ruled 6-3, that the act was unconstitutional because the tax was part of a plan to regulate agriculture, thus invading powers reserved to the states by the Tenth Amendment. The power to tax could not be used to achieve unconstitutional ends, such as regulating agriculture. Further, the tax on processors was not really a tax to raise revenue for the government; the money was specifically taken from processors to compensate farmers.
4. This decision was one factor leading to Roosevelt's confrontation with the Supreme Court. It was one of many New Deal programs struck down in 1935 and 1936. Another AAA went into effect in 1938, was challenged, and was found constitutional.

Evaluation of the Case

1. Answers will vary, but students today are accustomed to federal programs of this type.
2. Answers should show that students understand that the programs of the New Deal were a radical change in the amount of government interference in the economy, and that many of the justices had been appointed in earlier, more conservative times.
3. Answers will vary but should show that students have read and understood the relevant sections; this may help them understand how often Supreme Court decisions rest on interpretation.

Extending the Lesson

1. Have students research some of the specific programs authorized by the two Agricultural Adjustment Acts (1933 and 1938). What were their benefits? What were their failures? What farm programs from the Depression era are still in effect in modified form? You may want to have students broaden their research into a general look at the problems of the farm economy.
2. Subsidies to farmers in Europe, Japan, and elsewhere are a controversial issue in foreign trade today. Have a group of interested students research and report on what kinds of help foreign farmers receive from their government. How do these programs compare with U.S. farm policy?

United States v. Butler (1936)

Vocabulary

subsidy A grant given by the government to reduce the cost of something, such as land or a service.

receivers Those people appointed by a court to handle the money matters of a company in bankruptcy or other financial trouble.

Reviewing the Case

An important part of President Franklin D. Roosevelt's first New Deal program was the 1933 Agricultural Adjustment Act, which established the Agricultural Adjustment Administration (AAA). The act was intended to improve the farm economy by limiting farm production and thus raising prices on farm products. The agency worked with farmers to limit the number of acres of certain crops they cultivated, paying them for the acres they did not plant. In a few cases, crops that had been planted were destroyed and the farmers compensated for the loss. From most farmers' points of view, the AAA was a success. The government **subsidies** were so attractive to poor farmers suffering from the Depression that few farm families turned them down.

To pay for this program, Congress delegated to the Secretary of Agriculture the authority to impose and regulate a tax earmarked to pay for crop reduction benefits. The tax was imposed on the companies that processed agricultural products and readied them for market. The processors, in turn, were allowed to pass the cost of the tax on to consumers.

In the cotton industry, both a processing tax and a "floor stock" tax were imposed on cotton mills. The second tax applied to cotton that had been processed earlier and was on hand in the mill.

William Butler and others were **receivers** for a bankrupt New England cotton mill, the Hoosac Mills Corporation. They filed suit against the United States government in dis-

trict court, charging that the government had no constitutional right to tax the processors in order to pay cotton farmers for their losses. The government pointed out that Congress constitutionally has the power to levy taxes and raise money for the general welfare.

The district court ruled in favor of the government, but the circuit court of appeals reversed the decision and ruled in favor of Butler. The case then went to the United States Supreme Court. The issue then before the Court: Is the Agricultural Adjustment Act a constitutional use of the congressional power to tax?

The Court ruled by a 6–3 vote in favor of Butler, essentially finding the entire AAA statute unconstitutional. The majority interpretation was that the plan as a whole went beyond the constitutional authority of the federal government. In doing so, it invaded the powers reserved to the states by the Tenth Amendment. The tax itself was seen as part of a measure allowing federal regulation of agriculture. Congress could not use its powers to tax in order to achieve such unconstitutional ends.

Justice Owen J. Roberts wrote the majority opinion for the Court:

. . .[A]nother principle embedded in our Constitution prohibits the enforcement of the Agricultural Adjustment Act. The act invades the reserved rights of the states. It is a statutory plan to regulate and control agricultural production, a matter beyond the powers delegated to the federal government. The tax, the appropriation of the funds raised, and the direction for their disbursement, are but parts of the plan. They are but means to an unconstitutional end. . . .

In fact, the majority opinion said, the tax on the processors was not really a tax because the revenues did not go to the government. The money from the tax on processors was intended solely for the cotton farmers. Writing for the Court, Roberts denied that the money was in fact to be used for the general welfare:

> Beyond cavil the sole object of the legislation is to restore the purchasing power of agricultural products to a parity with that prevailing in an earlier day; to take money from the processor and bestow it upon farmers who will reduce their acreage. . . .
> . . .The tax plays an indispensable part in the plan of regulation. As stated by the Agricultural Adjustment Administrator, it is "the heart of the law." . . .

The three dissenting justices were Harlan Fiske Stone, Louis Brandeis, and Benjamin Cardozo. They all strongly defended the constitutionality of the AAA and the right of Congress to levy taxes and use the money in this way. Criticizing the majority opinion, Justice Stone called it a "tortured construction of the Constitution."

The *Butler* decision was a blow to the New Deal. It made relations much worse between the President and the mostly conservative Supreme Court and was a factor in his attempt the following year to change the make-up of the Court. Later in 1937, however, the Court began to uphold some New Deal legislation. In 1938, Congress rewrote the Agricultural Adjustment Act, and the second act was later ruled constitutional by the Court.

Name _____ Date _____

United States v. Butler (1936)

Elements of the Case

Directions: Fill in the appropriate information for each of the following elements of this case.

1. State the issue before the Supreme Court in this case.

_____
_____
_____
_____
_____

2. What facts of the case were presented to the Court?

_____
_____
_____
_____
_____

3. What was the decision of the Court? What was the rationale behind it?

_____
_____
_____
_____

4. What was the effect of the decision?

_____
_____
_____
_____

Evaluation of the Case

Directions: Use your own judgment to evaluate the justices' decision and state your opinion of that decision.

1. In your opinion, was this decision a proper one, considering the serious problems of the farm economy during the Depression? Explain.

_____

_____

_____

_____

_____

2. This was one of many New Deal programs found unconstitutional by the Supreme Court. What political motives might the majority justices have had in making these decisions? Explain.

_____

_____

_____

_____

3. The dissenting justices strongly criticized the limits that Roberts placed on Congress's right to tax. Read the Tenth Amendment, which protects the powers of the states, and Article 1, Section 8, which describes the powers granted to Congress. Do you agree with Roberts's interpretation that this agricultural program invaded the states' powers? Or with the government's argument that Congress was using its power to tax?

_____

_____

_____

_____

_____

Supreme Court Decision 27

Korematsu v. United States (1944)
Teacher Lesson Plan

Rationale

This lesson is designed to explore with students some of the ways in which World War II influenced American society and attitudes on the home front. This Supreme Court case involved an unsuccessful challenge to the presidential order that sent Japanese Americans to internment camps during World War II. Could wartime dangers justify the violation of their civil rights? Why were other Americans so fearful?

General Goals

This case study will provide students with opportunities to:

1. explore the challenges of American constitutional law
2. understand the processes and procedures of the judicial system
3. examine the role of the Supreme Court in the formation of public policy
4. explore the conflict between judicial activism and judicial restraint
5. examine the opinions of Supreme Court justices
6. demonstrate critical thinking skills

Directions

Student material is provided in four blackline masters on the following pages. These should be copied and distributed to students. They include a brief description of the *Korematsu* case as well as questions for students to answer.

Elements of the Case presents questions to check student comprehension, providing an opportunity to review with students the central issues, the Court's decision and rationale, and the effects of the case.

Evaluation of the Case provides one or more critical thinking activities for students. In this section, students are asked to evaluate the case and express their own positions on its issues.

Answer Key and Extending the Lesson

An answer key for the questions is provided on the next page, along with suggested activities for extending the lesson.

Korematsu v. United States (1944)

Answer Key

Elements of the Case

1. *Issue:* Are Executive Order #9066 and the act of Congress enforcing it constitutional uses of the war powers of the President and Congress?
2. The Japanese attack on Pearl Harbor aroused intense fears among people on the West Coast; civilians and military leaders were afraid of spying, sabotage, and even invasion. As a result, President Roosevelt issued an executive order setting up military areas in which military authorities had the power to remove or exclude whomever they wanted. The military authorities first put "all persons of Japanese ancestry" under a curfew, then ordered them relocated to camps away from the coast. An act of Congress made disobeying these orders a crime. Korematsu did not leave the restricted areas; he was discovered, arrested, convicted, and sent to a camp in Utah. He appealed his conviction to the court of appeals but lost.
3. The Supreme Court upheld Korematsu's conviction and said that military precautions and the need for quick action justified the executive order and the congressional act backing it up. The Court believed it was necessary to give the military unusual powers in wartime. The dissenting justices thought the actions were racist and unconstitutional.
4. As a result of the policy upheld in this case, about 112,000 Japanese-Americans were forced to spend the war years behind the barbed wire fences of remote and primitive camps in the West. Many lost pleasant homes and prospering farms and businesses. By the mid-1980s, more Americans were coming to believe that the incident had been racist to at least some extent. Under pressure, Congress author-ized the payment of damages to those who had been held in relocation camps.

Evaluation of the Case

1. Answers will vary, but most people today believe that the wholesale relocation of Japanese Americans was a shameful mistake, even in wartime.
2. Answers will vary, as many students will realize that so many Americans are of German or Italian descent that such relocation would have been impossible. Others will point out that, especially in the 1940s, it was easier for most Americans to see Asian Americans as "different" and "more foreign" than people of European descent.
3. Answers will vary, but students should realize that American society now is more accepting of many different racial and ethnic minority groups; in addition, there is more concern over human rights as well as more laws protecting against such discriminatory policies.

Extending the Lesson

1. Several memoirs of the relocation camps have been written by Japanese Americans, many focusing on the camp at Manzanar. Have students read and report on these or read selections from them aloud in class.
2. Have some students investigate what kinds of similar prejudicial attitudes and actions took place in American society during World War I. What kind of hostility did Americans of German descent face at that time? Have them describe their findings to the class or in a written report.
3. Have interested students or a small group research and report on some of the other related Supreme Court cases: *Hirabayashi v. United States*, *Ex parte Endo*, and the damage suits filed later.

Korematsu v. United States (1944)

Vocabulary

executive order A regulation or order issued by the President to enforce a treaty or law; it does not require congressional approval but has the force of law.

curfew A regulation requiring a certain group to be off the streets and in their homes at a certain time.

Reviewing the Case

After the Japanese bombing of Pearl Harbor in December 1941, the United States entered the war against the Axis powers—Germany, Italy, and Japan. The attack on Hawaii had made many American leaders and ordinary citizens increasingly fearful about security on the West Coast of the United States. In response to those fears, President Franklin D. Roosevelt issued **Executive Order** #9066 in February 1942.

The order authorized the creation of military areas in which military authorities had the power to remove or exclude whomever they wished. The first area included the entire West Coast to about 40 miles inland. Based on the executive order, military officials first imposed a **curfew** on "all persons of Japanese ancestry," including those born in the United States and those who had become citizens. Later, the military commander ordered all persons of Japanese ancestry to leave their homes and report to assembly centers. From there they were sent to relocation camps farther inland, away from the coast.

The government claimed the curfew and the relocations were necessary to prevent sabotage, spying, or giving help to a possible Japanese invasion force. Disobeying the military orders was made a crime by act of Congress. Several lawsuits were brought to challenge this violation of the civil rights of citizens.

Fred (Toyosaburo) Korematsu was arrested for staying in San Leandro, California, instead of going to a relocation center. Born in California, Korematsu was a defense-plant worker in his 20's. He had tried to join the Army but could not pass the physical. Rather than going to a center, he posed as Chinese. After being caught and arrested, he was convicted in federal district court of violating the military's "Civilian Exclusion Order." Conviction carried a maximum fine of $5,000 or up to one year in prison, or both.

Korematsu appealed the decision, unsuccessfully, to the Ninth Circuit Court of Appeals for California on the grounds that his rights under the Fourth, Fifth, Eighth, and Thirteenth Amendments had been violated. He was sent to a relocation camp in Utah. Korematsu then appealed to the U.S. Supreme Court.

The issue before the Court: Are Executive Order #9066 and the act of Congress enforcing it constitutional uses of the war powers of the President and Congress?

The Supreme Court ruled by a vote of 6–3 to uphold the decision of the lower courts against Korematsu. The Court ruled according to the precedent set a year earlier in *Hirabayashi v. United States*. Kiyoshi Hirabayashi had been convicted of violating the curfew law, which applied only to Japanese Americans. On appeal, the Court had ruled that Hirabayashi's rights had not been violated unconstitutionally because the curfew was within the limits of the war powers. In the interests of national security, the Court said, military authorities could do what they thought was necessary in sensitive areas; Congress had the right to give this power.

The Court's reasoning in both cases can be summed up in the words of Justice Hugo Black's opinion in *Korematsu*:

It should be noted, to begin with, that all legal restrictions which curtail the civil rights of a single racial group are immediately suspect. That is not to say that all such restrictions are unconstitutional. It is to say that courts must subject them to the most rigid scrutiny. . . . Compulsory exclusion of large groups of citizens from their homes, except under circumstances of direst emergency and peril, is inconsistent with our basic governmental institution. But when under conditions of modern warfare our shores are threatened by hostile forces, the power to protect must be commensurate [equal] with the threatened danger. . . .

The majority opinion stated that the quick judgments necessary during a war served as justification for the action, even though it brought hardships to many loyal people of Japanese descent. Continuing the majority opinion, Black denied that the policy had a racist intent:

Korematsu was not excluded from the Military Area because of hostility to him or his race. He was excluded because we are at war with the Japanese Empire, because the properly constituted military authorities feared an invasion of our West Coast and felt constrained to take proper security measures, because they decided that the military urgency of the situation demanded that all citizens of Japanese ancestry be segregated from the West Coast temporarily, and finally, because Congress, reposing its confidence in this time of war in our military leaders . . . determined that they should have the power to do just this.

The Court at the time did not rule on the constitutional issues and the questions of civil rights involved in these cases, only on the use of the war powers.

The three dissenting justices—Roberts, Murphy, and Jackson—thought that the policy was racist and unconstitutional. Justice Jackson feared that the decision gave the approval of the Constitution to an emergency military policy. The dissenting justices also pointed out that no effort had been made to identify individual Japanese Americans who might be disloyal, as had been done with some Germans and Italians. They claimed the policy violated the civil rights of an entire group of citizens solely on the basis of their ancestry.

As a result of this policy, about 112,000 Japanese Americans were forced to spend the war years behind the barbed wire fences of remote and primitive camps in the West. Many lost pleasant homes and prospering farms and businesses. President Harry Truman officially lifted the order in 1946, after the war was over. In the mid-1980's, more Americans were coming to believe that the incident had been racist to at least some extent. Under pressure, Congress authorized the payment of damages to those who had been held in relocation camps.

Name _____ Date _____

Korematsu v. United States (1944)

Elements of the Case

Directions: Fill in the appropriate information for each of the following elements of this case.

1. State the issue before the Supreme Court in this case.

_____

_____

_____

_____

2. What facts of the case were presented to the Court?

_____

_____

_____

_____

3. What was the decision of the Court? What was the rationale behind it?

_____

_____

_____

_____

4. What was the effect of the decision?

_____

_____

_____

_____

Supreme Court Decision 27

Evaluation of the Case

Directions: Use your own judgment to evaluate the justices' decision
and state your opinion of that decision.

1. In your opinion, did the Court make the right decision in this case?
   Explain why you agree or disagree.

_____

_____

_____

_____

_____

2. Do you think that German Americans and Italian Americans should
   have been relocated? Explain. Why do you suppose they were not?

_____

_____

_____

_____

_____

3. Do you think this action would be taken today in the event of a war?
   Explain.

_____

_____

_____

_____